Persuasive Programming

Jerud J. Mead

Bucknell University

Lewisburg, PA

Anil M. Shende

Roanoke College

Salem, VA

A|B|F Content • 8536 SW Saint Helens Drive, Suite D • Wilsonville, OR • 97070

President and Publisher	Jim Leisy (jimleisy@fbeedle.com)
Manuscript Editor	Tom Sumner
Proofreader	Jeni Lee
Cover Design	Ian Shadburne
Marketing	Chris Collier
Order Processing	Lois Allison
	Krista Hall
Manufacturing	Malloy Lithographing
	Ann Arbor, Michigan

Library of Congress Cataloging-in-Publication Data

Mead, Jerud J.
    Persuasive Programming / Jerud J. Mead, Anil M. Shende
        p. cm.
    ISBN 1-887902-60-0
    1. Computer programming. 2. Debugging in computer science. I. Shende, Anil M. II.
Title.
    QA76.6 .M428 2001
    005.2--dc21

                                                                00-065045

A|B|F Content is an imprint of Franklin, Beedle & Associates, Incorporated.

Preface

This set of lessons is guided by two overriding principles:

- programmers should understand why their programs behave as they do and
- their programs should explicitly express this understanding.

The following vignette reflects our motivation for developing these lessons.

Vignette – "Programming by Approximation"

Sam is anguishing over his first programming project – his code is up for review tomorrow and it's not quite ready. The code is pretty close, but

> "there's just this one last bug...and it seems to reside in this loop... What can be wrong with this thing? Maybe the loop bound is wrong – I'll change it.... Ah, that's a bit better, but the output still isn't quite right...maybe it's where I update i – I'll move that before this stuff.... Rats! Now nothing works.......... I'd better change that back."

And on he goes into the night.

Sam knows exactly what is expected of him – produce a code package which works and integrates correctly into the system. The programming style which Sam employs was learned in his student days and has proved to be successful. Unfortunately, the project he is working on now is much more complex than his student projects. Sam seems to understand that there is a relationship between changing the loop bound and the test output, but he doesn't (can't?) analyze exactly what the effect will be. In this programming style, which we call *programming by approximation*, the code is repeatedly manipulated in the hope that the next small modification will result in code which better approximates its specification. Through this process of "survival of the fittest," Sam's package evolves one modification at a time. In the end, Sam has a program whose execution approximates (or maybe meets) the specification; but now he must present the code for review, and he doesn't have a clear idea why it behaves as it does.

Okay – this picture is not entirely fair. Professional programmers have a good understanding of the semantics of the assignment and IO statements and even of simple selection statements and abstraction calls. But when it comes to more complex abstraction calls, selection, and especially repetition statements, semantic understanding is often fuzzy at best. This understanding is even fuzzier when the basic statement types are combined through nesting or sequencing. It would be nice if there were an analytical process which Sam could employ to understand the dynamics of the problematic loop.

Vignette – Writing vs. Programming

A few cubicles away from Sam, Sue is also hard at work on her part of the same project. She has run into similar coding problems and is well practiced in programming by approximation. Right now, she is working on a memo to her boss arguing for extra resources for her part of the project. Sue understands exactly what is expected of her. She knows that a simple statement of needs is not sufficient. She understands that the memo must include a statement of needs and a rationale, set in a logical framework, so that the memo stands on its own and the reader of the memo (i.e., her boss) is persuaded to honor the request. The style of writing which Sue employs is the *rhetorical* style of writing (we will use the term *persuasive*).

The interesting thing here is not that Sue understands how to write a persuasive memo. After all, her education groomed her for this activity, through what probably seemed like an endless sequence of essays and term papers. The interesting thing is that the persuasive style, which is so successful for proving a point, is not also employed when writing programs. It is not employed for writing programs because her boss doesn't expect it to be employed. Sue's education also groomed her to program by approximation and not persuasively.

Vignette – Why Comment?

Sam, our intrepid programmer, has finally gotten the code to work! Now the final task.

> "Finally done!! Now, where is that coding standard I'm supposed to use..."

What Sam produces in the end will utilize a consistent naming strategy, possibly pre- and post-conditions with function definitions, and then some comments in the code. Here is a sample function definition which might appear in Sam's program:

```
//*******************************************************
//******************* insert ************************
//*******************************************************
void insert(List list, int value) {
  // pre: list is a list and value is an integer
  // post: value is inserted in list

  int X = 0;  // X is loop counter initialized to 0

  ...
  //  this loop inserts "value" in "list"
  while(...) {...
      ...
      X = X + 1;   // increment X by 1
      ...
  }
}
```

So what kinds of comments do we have here? The pre- and post-conditions are
welcome, but they don't really convey information not already implied by the
function's name. Where is the value inserted? Is the list sorted before insert
is called? After? And the comment before the repetition statement seems to
be more a hope than a statement of fact. The comment on the assignment
statement is welcome because it is an attempt to represent the semantics of
the commented statement. But the semantics of this particular assignment
statement is so simple that the comment is redundant. What comment do you
suppose accompanied the problematic loop of the first vignette?

In Defense of Programming by Approximation

The comments above present programming by approximation in a bad light.
But, in fact, programming by approximation is the only real option, unless we
expect every bit of code to be correct on first writing. So what's the problem? In
the first vignette Sam bases his next modification on intuition and hope rather
than on analysis.

A Persuasive Style of Programming

For years programming students have been fed a diet of formal syntax and
very informal semantics. They have been encouraged to write nicely formatted
programs with imprecise comments documenting primarily the structure of the
code rather than its semantics. These problems naturally carry over to the programmer's professional life. The problems illustrated by the vignettes above are
a consequence not of focusing too much on syntax, but rather of not focusing
enough on semantics. A better grounding in semantics might give Sam a base
from which to seek a solution for his loop problem; in fact, a better semantic

understanding might have allowed Sam to avoid that problem from the start. What about Sue's situation? Her boss expects a persuasive memo, but not a persuasive program. Why? Shouldn't her boss expect as much from a program as from a memo? And the comments in Sam's program? More focus on semantics might allow Sam to include detailed indications of semantic effects.

The purposes of this set of lessons are

- to provide support for directing attention toward the semantic side, and

- to bring the tradition of rhetorical writing to the programming process.

The vehicle for this redirection is *persuasive programming*, an approach which focuses on content rather than form. The style makes use of assertions to reflect properties of a program's state (i.e., semantic content) at selected locations in a program's text. By including the assertions, the programmer's attention is naturally drawn toward the semantic side while designing and writing the program. The result is code which carries its own "persuasive argument" of validity.

Admittedly, the use of assertions is not new. They have been used formally and informally for years, and many programming languages provide some support for their use. What is new is the persuasive programming style: a systematic, semantically based approach to the use of assertions. These lessons present the persuasive style by integrating the use of assertions with a state-based introduction to statement semantics.

The persuasive programming style is not program correctness dressed up with a new name. Program correctness requires a proof – formal, complete, and correct. Persuasive programming requires only that evidence of correctness accompany the program code – not necessarily a proof. What is nice about persuasive programming, however, is that it can be the first step towards producing a provably correct program.

Learning Persuasive Programming

There are two aspects to persuasive programming: the semantics of program statements and the integration of the semantics into the text of a program. Our approach to presenting statement semantics is to determine for each statement type a pattern of assertions which describes the semantics. We start with the most obvious pattern (often rather clumsy) and then, by analyzing examples, work toward more useful patterns. When asserting a program the programmer should always be able to rely on the pattern for the particular statement. The analysis of the original pattern has two purposes: to determine clearer and more concise patterns and, perhaps more importantly, to help programmers develop the ability to analyze the semantics of their own program statements.

Integrating the statement semantics into a program's text is what persuasive programming is all about. How does a programmer learn to balance the assertional comments with program clarity? The persuasive programming style should not be taught; rather, it should be experienced by programmers in every piece of code they see and write. If they see enough of the style, they will come to see it as the natural way of programming.

Of course, for the style to be convincing, it must not be seen as rigid and restrictive. The style presented in example code must be seen as adapting to the programer's increasing semantic sophistication. Simple statements which were carefully asserted in early examples may go unasserted in later examples. On the programmer side, writing good assertions is not easy. The persuasive style requires a new language – the language of state-based semantics – and it must be studied and practiced.

Using the Text

The text is designed for flexible use. The basic sub-divisional unit has been called a *Lesson* because our expectation (and experience) is that the material, if presented in a classroom setting, could be covered in one class period. But the text is also written in a tutorial style, so it is convenient for self-paced study.

The text is in three parts. *Part I* comprises four lessons and introduces the idea of persuasive programming. Lessons 1 and 2 cover the basics of programming language syntax and semantics and introduce important concepts such as state and state change. Lessons 3 and 4 present the semantics of simple statement structures including expressions, assignment statement, and IO statements. *Part II*, Lessons 5 – 9, extends the persuasive style to include the standard high-level programming structures: sequencing (Lesson 5), selection (Lesson 6), repetition (Lesson 7), and abstraction (Lesson 8). For each structure, an analytical process is developed for determining statement semantics and writing appropriate assertions. Lesson 9 presents an extended example. *Part III* is a reprise of *Part II*. Lesson 10 is a discussion of first-order assertions and their application to algorithms involving arrays. Lessons 11 – 13 give second, more in-depth discussions of selection (Lesson 11), repetition (Lesson 12), and abstraction (recursion) (Lesson 13). Lesson 14 presents two extended examples.

The three *Parts* should be covered in order. In *Part I*, the lessons form a sequence. In *Part II*, the middle three lessons (6, 7, 8) are independent and can be covered in any order; for example, the discussions and examples of Lesson 8 contain no code involving selection or repetition statements. This independence means the reader can concentrate on the semantics of the particular statement type without the complication of other statement types. *Part III* has a structure like *Part II*, though since all lessons of *Part III* assume knowledge of *Part II*, the middle three lessons may appear to be less independent, though they are. The diagram below represents the precedence graph for the fourteen lessons of the text.

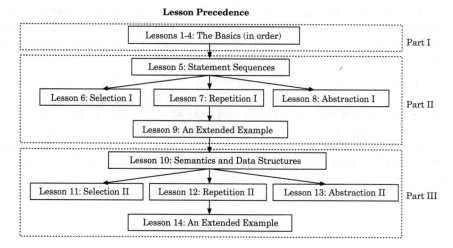

Acknowledgments

Many people and organizations were instrumental in bringing this project to fruition. Participants in our 1997 National Science Foundation (NSF)-sponsored workshop critiqued an early draft of this text, giving us encouragement and direction. From that group John Derrick and Carl Bredlau have provided both friendship and valuable feedback on subsequent versions of the text as well — for this the authors are grateful. The advice, support, and commentary of Gary Haggard has also been invaluable. We also want to thank Roanoke College students Gus Scheidt and Ben Hosp for their comments and help with typesetting. During the project, we have been generously supported by our respective institutions, Bucknell University and Roanoke College, and the NSF.

Many thanks to Jim Leisy, President of Franklin, Beedle & Associates, whose belief in, and commitment to, our project made it possible to bring this book into being. Our thanks also go out to Tom Sumner, Managing Editor at Franklin, Beedle & Associates, for setting us straight on our punctuation and working with us on the layout of the manuscript.

The authors have been inspired by works of others. David Riley's book *Using Pascal: An Introduction to Computer Science* (Boyd & Fraser, 1987) makes extensive use of assertions for representing the semantics of statements; his ideas are at the heart of this text. David Gries, in his book *The Science of Programming* (Springer-Verlag, 1981), showed the benefits of the conscious application of knowledge and principles to programming. Roland Barthe, the 20th-century French intellectual, reminded us through his writings of the centrality of rhetoric in written communication.

Finally, the authors want to pay tribute to their families, Anil to his wife Susheela and daughter Maya, and Jerry to his wife Jane and his sons Andrew and Nathan, for their patience and understanding while the project was underway. Without their support and understanding this text would have languished long ago.

Contents

Part I

Basics

Lesson 1

Introduction

Language is an integral part of being human. The languages we speak each day, so-called *natural* languages, have evolved over the millions of years of human development and are used for both external communication with others and for internal communication with ourselves, for scientific reasoning and emotional expression. Each natural language has its own particular form, with certain acceptable sounds and sound sequences – *syntax* – and associated meanings – *semantics*.

The interesting thing about a natural language is that it is inherently *personal*. There may be general agreement among members of a family, a group of friends, or a culture on the meaning of a particular word or phrase, but each of us adds nuances which derive from our personal experiences. When we speak we must be aware that our words may be interpreted by the listener in ways we did not intend, possibly in very subtle ways. This, of course, is because we cannot be completely aware of the personal context within which the listener interprets our words.

In contrast, programming languages are inherently *impersonal*. What do we mean by that? The fundamental purpose of a programming language is to communicate to a computer a sequence of instructions for the computer to carry out. The computer, rather than a human being, is the interpreter of a particular instruction and the interpretation is ultimately determined by the internal circuitry on a silicon chip so there can be no ambiguity, no unknowable added nuance. Since the internal physical structure of a computer is known, the interpretation of each instruction is known.

To understand programming, then, requires some understanding of how a computer will ultimately interpret the programs we write. But beyond that understanding is the ability to convince oneself or others, for that matter, that a particular program does what it is supposed to do – i.e., the program is correct. In these lessons we will develop a rhetoric for programming – a style of persuasive programming – which, if employed, will help you to write programs which contain the evidence they are correct.

3

Using Language for Problem Solving

The roots of programming are "lost in the mists of time," as they say. But we do find evidence in the artifacts of ancient cultures of verbal descriptions of how to solve problems. The Rhind Papyrus (circa 1650 BC) is evidence that the ancient Egyptians used written language for such descriptive purposes. And they were not alone; the Babylonians developed written solutions to mathematical problems in the same time frame. Algebraic notation, which we all study in junior and senior high school as a language for solving certain classes of mathematical problems, has its origins in seventh century Islamic culture.

The specialized notations used to describe solutions to problems have, until very recently, evolved in an *ad hoc* manner, with conventions of form and meaning developing through mutual agreement over long periods of time. Such problem solutions can be characterized as sequences or lists of computational instructions, for example:

> *"Set the discount to the cost of the item multiplied by the discount factor."*

> *"Knit 2, purl 2: Repeat across each row until the work is 2 inches long."*

The second example illustrates that in some settings the term "computational" must be taken figuratively. Whatever the form, generations of problem solvers have learned to translate the solution description, in the form of an algebraic expression or a list of knitting instructions, into the correct sequence of basic computational actions which the problem solver can follow to produce a specific solution.

The Advent of Computers

Over time, advances in computational techniques have made it possible to solve increasingly complex problems. Unfortunately, the old, familiar, *ad hoc* description methods, although they may be more structured and formal, are still subject to the same problems of inconsistency and ambiguity that plague the use of natural languages in a conversational setting. When problem solutions are not too complex, these ambiguities and inconsistencies can be ironed out, but with complex solutions the question of "what do they mean by that?" occurs more frequently and is more difficult to resolve.

With the advent of computers, the range of problems for which solutions are sought has grown dramatically. The big advantage that computers bring to the problem-solving arena is a completely known internal language structure — the computer's *machine language*[1], which is present in the form of the central processing unit (CPU). Not only are all the terms (instruction forms) of a

---

[1] A computer's machine language is, in fact, a numeric code based on the binary numbers; i.e., using only the digits 0 and 1.

machine language known, but the way in which each term is interpreted by the machine is also known. This level of understanding is not currently possible for the natural languages.

While the machine language of a computer is a fine language for the computer, it is a difficult language for people to use in any practical way.[2] For this reason programming languages have been developed to bridge the gulf between our own natural language and the computer's internal machine language. Programming languages are artificial languages with rigid syntax and semantics and solve two fundamental problems related to computer-based problem solving:

1. Programming languages are sufficiently close to our *ad hoc* language for describing problem solutions, so a person can convert an *ad hoc* solution description into an *equivalent*[3] program in the programming language.

2. Programming languages are sufficiently close to the machine language so it is possible to automatically translate a solution description (in the programming language) into an equivalent machine language program. The automatic translation is carried out by programs called *interpreters* and *compilers.*

The Fundamental Problem of Programming

Remember that earlier we said a fundamental problem for the speaker of a natural language is to speak a phrase which will evoke in the listener the same meaning as for the writer. The programmer has a similar problem. A problem needs solving and the computer is ultimately going to do the solving. The programmer must determine a solution, through an internal dialog (possibly with the help of co-workers), and then translate the solution into an appropriate form using a programming language. (Notice that this solution is initially derived in the programmer's native natural language.)

Now things get serious! How can the programmer be sure that the program produced actually describes the same solution developed in the natural language? This may not sound like a big deal, but if the problem is to control and monitor a nuclear power plant or an industrial waste disposal system, the programmer wants to be very sure the description is right. In other words, the programmer wants to be sure that the meaning he/she has "in mind" for the program is, in fact, the one that is inherently present in the program he/she has written.

---

[2]Even though machine language is difficult for humans to deal with, programmers of the earliest computers did their programming directly in machine language.

[3]By equivalent we mean if the computer follows the instructions in the program, it will come up with the same answers the person would come up with if the *ad hoc* instructions were followed.

> ### The Fundamental Principle
> ### of
> ### Programming
>
> A program is a description of a solution to a particular problem.

> ### The Fundamental Problem
> ### of
> ### Programming
>
> How does one tell if a particular program describes a solution for a given problem?

These two statements summarize the focus of this text. We will now turn to a more detailed look at the basic characteristics of programming languages and how they relate to **The Fundamental Principle/Problem of Programming**.

1.1   Characteristics of Programming Languages

The study of any language revolves around three fundamental questions:

1. What are the basic building blocks of the language ("words" and special symbols)?

2. How are building blocks combined into "phrases" and then into "sentences" (programs)?

3. What meanings are associated with phrases and sentences (programs) of the language?

Answers to the first two questions describe a language's *syntax* or form, while answers to the third describe a language's *semantics*. These notions of syntax and semantics should be familiar to you, as you have had to deal with them in the natural languages you have learned. Since you are reading this book you either already know or are currently learning yet another language, but this time an *artificial* one. What do the terms *syntax* and *semantics* mean for an *artificial* language such as C^{++} [4]? Are the questions even meaningful? It should be clear

---

[4] While the examples and illustrations in this book are specific to the language C^{++}, the principles apply to all imperative programming languages.

that an artificial language such as C^{++} has a syntax structure; after all, you have already seen a few programs and the regularity of their forms should be clear. But what about semantics? Can a statement in a C^{++} program have a meaning? Can a program have a meaning? The purpose of these lessons is to investigate the answer to this question and to learn how an understanding of semantics can help make you a more effective programmer.

Before moving on we should identify four basic elements which we find present in natural langauge problem solutions and which, not surprisingly, we find reflected in programming languages. Three of the elements represent the static and dynamic sides of data in a problem solution, while the fourth relates to the sequencing of the steps in a solution. We use the following step extracted from a problem solution to illustrate the first three elements:

> *"Set the discount to the cost of the item multiplied by the discount factor."*

One element is static references to data, as seen in the use of names, such as

> *"cost of the item"* and *"discount factor,"*

and expressions, such as

> *"cost of the item multiplied by the discount factor."*

In both of these cases values are described which are unknown at the time a solution description is written. In programming-language parlance these names and expressions are said to be *declarative* elements of the language. The second element is also declarative in nature and relates to the definition of the names used in a solution. Definitions are not always present because the informal nature of solution descriptions often assume the reader will intuitively know the attributes associated with the names in use. Certainly in the step quoted above it is clear that *"cost of the item"* refers to a currency amount and *"discount factor"* refers to a non-negative fractional value. But definitions stating these assumptions for the names could have been included in the solution description.

The third element relates to the dynamic (*imperative*, in programming language terms) side of data and is seen as any element dealing with data movement. This is illustrated in the previous extracted step by the phrase

> *"Set the discount to...."*

The implication is that the value described by the expression is to be moved to or associated with the name *"discount."* This is clearly a different way of using a name than the declarative ways discussed in the previous paragraph.

Finally we come to the fourth element of problem solution descriptions, which also falls into the category of imperative elements. To illustrate this fourth element we look at a different example: the knitting instruction we saw at the beginning of this lesson.

> *"Knit 2, purl 2: Repeat across each row until the work is 2 inches long."*

In this instruction one term in particular stands out – *repeat*. This term implies that a certain sequence of steps is to be carried out, then to be carried out again, and again, until a certain condition is met (*"the work is 2 inches long."*). This is an example of *sequencing* – i.e., specifying the sequence in which a set of steps is to be carried out. The term *"repeat"* is interesting here because it does not deal directly with data, but influences the order in which data will be manipulated. If we look at the two imperative elements, the first, associating a value with a name, is a single indivisible instruction (at least at the high level of this specification), while the *repeat* instruction is one that combines other instructions into a unit. We say that the *repeat* instruction is a *high-level* instruction.

To summarize, we have identified four elements of solution descriptions, two declarative and the other two imperative.

declarative
> name definitions – associate attributes with names
> data references – access to data

imperative
> indivisible instructions
> high-level (sequencing) instructions

In the next section we will look at the basic syntactic structure of a programming language and see where these four elements appear.

1.2   Programming Language Syntax

The syntax for a language defines which symbols and sequences of symbols constitute phrases and sentences in the language. In the case of a programming language, the phrases of the language are the expressions and program statements and the sentences of the language are the complete programs. The syntax of a programming language, as implied by the first two questions above, can be specified at two levels. At the lower, *lexical* level are the words and special symbols, what we call the *lexical elements* (sometimes called *tokens*). At the higher, *grammatical* level are the phrases and sentences (expressions, statements, and programs) of the language.

The syntactic structure of an artificial language must, by necessity, be formalizable – i.e., it must be possible to precisely describe all lexical and grammatical elements of the language. We say "by necessity" because artificial languages are meant to be processed in some automatic way, for example by computer. If the syntax of the language cannot be described completely, then it will not be possible to instruct a computer what constitutes a legal sentence of the artificial language.

Lexical Level

The lexical elements of C^{++}, analogous to the words and punctuation symbols of a natural language, can be split into four categories.

Key Words These are names set aside and associated with predefined uses in the language.

Identifiers These are names whose meanings are defined by the program in which they occur.

Literals A literal represents a data value where the value represented is apparent from the form of the literal – "123" is a literal which represents the integer value *one-hundred and twenty three* – a lexical element which is to be understood literally.

Special Symbols Special symbols are either punctuation symbols, which serve to mark the boundaries of sequences of lexical symbols, or symbols which act as operations, such as the arithmetic operation symbols.

The following table gives samples of the lexical elements of C^{++} from these different categories.

Key Words	Identifiers	Literals	Special Symbols
class	Value	123	.
int	Value5	-37.43	;
return	I.y	"Enter Value"	::
break	HowMany		*
while			/
if			[
case			]
new			,

Selected Lexical Elements of C^{++}

Since the sets of key words and special symbols are fixed, we can describe them by just listing them. The identifiers follow a simple formation rule: an identifier must start with a letter and can be followed by a (finite) sequence of letters, digits, and a particular set of special symbols – that's easy. The literals have similarly easy descriptions.

Grammatical Level

At the grammatical level, the structure of C^{++} is more complex. The earlier statement that syntax "must be [...] formalizable" really means formalizable from a mathematical point of view. But the formal mathematical description can also be accurately described using easily understood diagrams (called railroad diagrams). In fact, a check through almost any C^{++} text will uncover diagrams describing the syntactic structure. The grammatical structure of the C^{++} syntax can be broken down into four categories, based on the declarative and imperative elements described above.

1. identifier definitions – declarative

2. expressions – declarative

3. simple statements (input, output, assignment) – imperative

4. high-level statements (selection, repetition, abstraction) – imperative

The following is a C^{++} program that inputs two integer values and displays their sum. The first three grammatical categories are represented in this program; only the high-level statement category is not represented.

```
int main () {

    float Sum;
    int    Num1,
           Num2;

    cin >> Num1;
    cin >> Num2;

    Sum = Num1 + Num2;

    cout << Sum << endl;
}
```

The first three code lines after the `main` line are declarative statements and serve to define the names `Sum`, `Num1`, and `Num2`. A definition always associates a set of attributes with a name – in these cases, the definitions associate a data type (either `int` or `float`) with each name.

Each of the next four code lines is an imperative statement, the first two being input statements, the third an assignment statement, and the fourth an output statement. Of particular note in these imperative statements are the elements which are underlined. In each case, the underlined element represents a value to be determined – we call each of these elements an expression, even the simple identifiers. The identifiers which are *not* underlined do not represent values to be used, but rather represent a "location" where a new value will be saved.

1.3   Programming Language Semantics

The semantics for a language associates a meaning with words, phrases, and sentences of the language. While there are various techniques for describing the syntactic structure of a programming language in a complete, clear, and concise way, a complete description of its semantics can be specified only with some difficulty and at the cost of clarity.[5] There are, however, important reasons for wanting a complete and formal description of the semantics for a programming language.

1. Any programmer who writes a compiler or interpreter for a programming language needs a formal description of semantics so that the program can be translated into appropriate actions.

2. A programmer writing a program that will control a critical system, such as a nuclear power plant or intensive-care system, needs to be able to guarantee that the program he/she has written is correct. The formal description of semantics can be used to prove the program correct.

3. Researchers make use of formal semantic descriptions to investigate new languages and new language features.

Our interest in semantics is not so formal. We will investigate the basic notions of programming language semantics without getting bogged down in formalism and, based on these investigations, will develop techniques to improve the programming process. The techniques will be the basis for the persuasive programming style that is the central focus of these lessons.

In the context of programming language we can say that semantics relates to change. The perception of change, however, relies on an environment within which the change occurs. If we think of a person running the program above, the relevant environment would seem to be the keyboard, where the input values are typed, and the video screen, where the result is displayed. Things definitely change in the person's environment – the data that is input is "consumed" by the program and the output appears. But the programmer will have a different perception of the changes which result from running the program because the programmer knows the instructions being executed. If we look at what changes for the programmer the answer is fairly clear – the identifiers in the program (these identifiers all name variables) represent storage space for data values – and the values associated with the identifiers change as the program executes. For this reason we focus on the identifiers in a program when we talk about the programmer's environment for the program.

To be a bit more precise, the programmer's environment is defined by the definition statements in the program; these declarative statements establish an environment of identifier/attribute associations – we will refer to these as *identifier/attribute pairs*. It is this environment that changes as the program executes, though it is not the attributes that change, just the values associated with the identifiers. It is useful to emphasize these two important aspects of the program environment.

---

[5]The difficulty and loss of clarity result from the fact that formal descriptions of semantics make use of advanced mathematical techniques. This makes these descriptions inaccessible to most programmers.

1. The environment is *static* and is represented by the set of identi-fier/attribute pairs derived from the declarative statements.[6]

2. The environment is *dynamic* and is seen at runtime as the set of name/value pairs.

At runtime the name/value pairs are referenced and modified through the execution of the imperative statements. At runtime we refer to the dynamic environment as the program's *state*. The basic notion of semantics comes from this change of the program's state as the program executes.

---

[6]We will discuss later, in Lesson 3.1, that the set of valid name/attribute pairs *can* change during execution.

Lesson 2

Semantics – Perspective Matters

The notion of semantics in the context of programming languages is not a simple one, but it is a manageable one. In order to gain a solid understanding of the principles and how to put them to practical use in the persuasive programming style, it is important to closely examine the basic notions on which semantics depends. In this lesson we will motivate and define the notions of program environment and state as seen by the user of a program and as seen by the programmer. These two perspectives are critical and will lead to important definitions for program specification (intended semantics), program semantics (inherent semantics), and program correctness, which links intended and inherent semantics.

This lesson assumes that you have been introduced to the basic structure of a C^{++} program and also to the standard C^{++} input and output statements based on cin and cout.

2.1 Program Environment

The appropriate definition for program environment may seem pretty clear at this point, especially since in the previous section we indicated that the environment of a program consists of the identifiers defined in the program's declarative statements. Well, that was not quite the whole picture — there are some additional factors which play a major role in the notion of program environment and, consequently, in the notion of program semantics.

One important point to remember while deriving an appropriate definition of program environment is that there are two relevant vantage points from which to "view" the environment of a program. If we take the programmer's view, then the obvious conclusion is that the environment is the set of items defined by the program's declarative statements – we call this view the *programmer's environment*. But by taking into account the user's view of the program, what

13

we will call the *user's environment*, we will get a more complete notion of program environment and, in addition, gain a bit of insight into the programming process.

The User's View of Environment

Since we believe that program semantics hinges on the idea of how a program's environment changes, we might ask what the user perceives as changing when a program executes. One thing that usually changes is the video screen: the program produces a sequence of data values which are displayed in the user's actual physical environment. We call this sequence of data values, which seems to flow from the program, the program's *output stream*. As the program executes, the data on the output stream doesn't appear all at once, rather, it accumulates a little (or perhaps a lot) at a time.

In the opposite "direction," the program takes a sequence of data values from the user's environment into the program's (internal) environment for processing. We call this sequence of data values, which seems to flow into the program, the program's *input stream*. As with the output stream, the data values on the input stream are not consumed by the running program all at once, but rather a few at a time. In fact, when a program is running we will consider the input stream (at a particular time) to be the sequence of data values which are yet to be consumed by the program.

Environment of a Program
– user's view –

The *environment* of a program, from the user's view, consists of

1. the input stream and

2. the output stream.

Okay, it's true that most real programs are more complex than just single input and output streams. A web browser, for example, takes input from the keyboard, a pointing device (mouse), and the network — at least three separate input streams. The same can be said for output streams.

The Programmer's View of Environment

The programmer's view of the program environment is represented by the identifiers defined by the program's declarative statements. Each identifier defined in a declaration statement names an item in the programmer's environment. What actually comprises an item in the environment will be discussed in Section 3.1.

But this isn't the entire picture. Since the programmer must specify how input data is consumed and how output data is produced, the input and output streams must also be in the programmer's view of the program environment. Actually, this should come as no surprise. The reason C^{++} programs include the file `iostream.h` is so that the input and output streams can be named. The standard identifiers `cin` and `cout`, defined in `iostream.h`, name the program's actual connections to the user's physical environment. There will be more detail about these in the next lesson.

There is one final, rather subtle, thing which changes during the execution of the program: the identification of the next statement to be executed. We will assume that there is a hidden value associated with each program called the *program counter*, denoted as `PC`. We will also assume that each statement of the program has a unique number associated with it (e.g., a line number). As the program executes, the value of `PC` is always the number of the next statement to be executed, i.e., when a statement is executed the value of `PC` is automatically updated.[1] With this final component in place we can summarize the programmer's view of the program environment.

Environment of a Program
– programmer's view –

The *environment* of a program consists of

1. the input stream,

2. the output stream,

3. the PC, and

4. the set of all program identifiers.

2.2   Semantics for the User

The user has an interesting perspective from which to understand a program. First, the user can see how the input and output streams change as the program executes. But the user also has an expectation of how the input and output streams *should* change. These two related ideas are the *inherent semantics* (what the user sees) and the *intended semantics* (what the user expects). An example will help clarify these two semantic flavors.

---

[1]This `PC` is analogous to the program counter register in a processor. The fact that the `PC` always holds the number of the next statement to execute may seem strange, but this characteristic of a program counter is a technical requirement.

Example 1 – Specifying a simple program

▼

The owner of a business would like to have a program developed which will help with bookkeeping. Being unsure of what exactly the program should do, the owner decides to start modestly with a prototype which will simply input two values and print their sum. The firm's programmer is given the task of producing the program, which is to be called `Add`. The programmer sees no problem.

> *"Input two reals and output the sum? No problem!"*

The next day the owner tries out the first version of `Add` which the programmer proudly presents. Here is the appearance of the screen after the first test session.

```
12.34 13.45
25.79
```

The owner is underwhelmed!

> *"This isn't at all what I expected!"*

Of course, the owner immediately sees the problem and writes out the following description for the concerned programmer.

> *The program should first display the following prompt on the screen*
>
> > *Enter two (real) values >>*
>
> *to which the user will respond by typing two real values. Then the program will print out on the next line the sum like this.*
>
> > *The sum of the values is 25.79*
>
> *assuming that numbers like 12.34 and 13.45 were entered.*

The programmer, relieved to still have a job, now completely understands what is expected (*"Why couldn't I have been told in the first place?"*) and returns shortly with the program the owner described.

▲

   In this example the owner has a user's view of the program, and the programmer apparently didn't understand that. The interesting thing to notice from this simple example is that the first program produced by the programmer did work, it just wasn't what the owner expected. To avoid the same problem in the future, the owner needs a more specific, more structured approach to specifying programs. What the owner could have done is to ask the programmer to create a program that would indicate the status of the input and output streams initially and then when the program terminates.

Formally, we refer to the status of the input and output streams before and after execution as the *initial state* and the *final state* of the program. For the program in the example we have the following situation:[2]

initial state: input stream: $< v_1, v_2 >$
                 output stream: empty

final state: input stream: empty
                 output stream: `Enter two (real) values >>`
                                  `The sum of the values is` $v1 + v2$

There is one thing here which you might find a bit odd. According to this representation the initial state of the input stream is not empty. How can this be? Presumably no data will be input until the program prints a prompt directing the user to do so. The answer is one of convenience. While it is true that the input stream is initially empty, in this program we know that eventually the user will enter two data values. It is easier to describe or analyze a program when the input stream is initialized in this way – we will use this technique frequently in the coming lessons.

The initial and final states of a program are just two specific instances of a more general concept. The *state* of a program at a particular time consists of the values associated with the input and output streams at that time. The input stream is not emptied all at once by the program; rather, there is an *input/output* cycle during which data values are read from the input stream and new data is written to the output stream. Notice that the time for a particular state may be before the program begins executing (the initial state) or some time after the program begins to execute but before it terminates. A simple example will illustrate this input/output cycle.

Example 2 – Enhancing the program
▼

Our business owner recognizes that just reporting the simple sum of the two input values may not always be enough – there are times when a rounded value rather than just the straight sum will be needed. The owner wants the programmer to enhance the program so that after entering the two values the user will enter a third value indicating whether to print the straight sum or a rounded (integer) value. Recognizing that this program is more complex than the first, the owner decides on a new strategy.

1. Make it clearer how the user should see the data on the screen change by specifying a new program state for each change to either the input or output stream.

---

[2]We need to point out that, though the values $v1$ and $v2$ are typed by the user, the values are not part of the output of the program – the computer system "echoes" these keystrokes to the screen. They appear to be part of the output, but in fact are not.

2. The behavior of the program is dependent on the third value in the input stream, so specify different possible final states depending on the third value.

The owner finds the resulting description to be very satisfactory.

`State`

`initial:`   input stream: $< v_1, v_2, a >$
                output stream: empty

`1st:`   input stream: $< v_1, v_2, a >$
                output stream: `Enter two (real) values >>`

`2nd:`   input stream: $< a >$
                output stream: `Enter two (real) values >>`

`3rd:`   input stream: $< a >$
                output stream: `Enter two (real) values >>`
                                `Round the answer?  (y/n) >>`

`4th:`   input stream: empty
                output stream: `Enter two (real) values >>`
                                `Round the answer?  (y/n) >>`

If the value of a is 'y', then the final state is given as follows, with $R(v1 + v2)$ indicating that the sum is rounded.

input stream: empty
output stream: `Enter two (real) values >>`
                    `Round the answer?  (y/n) >>`
                    `The sum of the values is` $R(v1 + v2)$

If the value of a is 'n', then the final state is given as follows:

input stream: empty
output stream: `Enter two (real) values >>`
                    `Round the answer?  (y/n) >>`
                    `The sum of the values is` $v1 + v2$

And if the value of a is any other character, then the final state is given as follows:

input stream: empty
output stream: `Enter two (real) values >>`
                  `Round the answer?  (y/n) >>`
                  `Invalid response - please run again.`

A couple of points about the first through fourth states: Notice that from the first state to the second state, both values v1 and v2 are consumed from the input stream, leaving only the value a. The third results from the execution of an output statement, so only the output stream is altered. The fourth state, of course, results from the input of the value a, leaving an empty input stream.

▲

This notion of program state is quite useful and leads to two new concepts.

1. **Intended Semantics (Program Specification)**

   By giving the desired initial, intermediate, and final states, we have defined the behavior required of the program *before* the program is written. We call this the program's *inherent semantics* – also in common use is the term *program specification*.

2. **Inherent (User) Semantics**

   When the initial, intermediate, and final states of an executing program are observed, the user is seeing the changes to the (user's) program environment due to the execution of the program. We refer to these changes in the (user's) program environment as the *intended semantics* of the program.

From what we have just said it would seem that these two notions of intended and inherent semantics are identical — so why distinguish them? In an ideal world this might be true, but in fact, given a specification for a program, a programmer will often misinterpret part of the specification and produce a program whose semantics don't match the specification (remember our first example) – the program is *not right*. Actually, it might be better to say that the program is *not the right one*. The program may be a very nice program which handles all the special cases and does not crash, but if the semantics do not match the specification, it means the programmer wrote the wrong program – remember the experience in Example 1. The goal is for the semantics of the program to be the same as the specification for the program: when this is true we say the program is correct.

Program Correctness

A program is *correct* if the inherent semantics of the program are the same as the intended semantics (specification) for the program.

2.3   Semantics for the Programmer (What is State?)

When a program is executing, changes take place in the programmer's environment as well. But in the programmer's environment, besides the input and output streams, there are objects that change. In particular, the PC (program counter) and variables change. The notion of state introduced in the last section can be extended in a very natural way to the programmer's environment.[3]

State of a Program

The *state* of a program at a particular time consists of

1. the sequence of values remaining in the input stream,

2. the sequence of values in the output stream, and

3. the set of variable/value pairs for the program's environment, including the PC.

So the environment is static and defined by the declarative statements in a program, while the state is dynamic and reflects changes within the environment caused by the execution of the imperative statements. We can now state our basic definition of the semantics for a program, based on the notions of environment, state, and change.

---

[3]In the remainder of these lessons we will be primarily interested in the programmer's view of things, so we will always discuss environment, state, and semantics from the programmer's view. This is not really a restriction, since the user's view of a program is a subset of the programmer's view.

Semantics of a Program

The *semantics of a program* is the change in the state of the program due to the execution of that program.

This definition reflects the semantics of a program taken as a unit. But as programmers, we really want to know what happens *during* the execution of the program. For this we need to broaden our notion of semantics to include imperative statements. If we can formalize what we mean by the semantics for each statement in a program, then we should be able to link the initial and final states of the program to demonstrate that a program does what is intended. The remainder of this section and the sections which follow focus on this important idea of statement semantics.

2.4 What Changes State?

As a customer ordering a specially designed piece of software, the definition given above for the semantics of a program would be quite satisfactory. The customer would be most interested in how the program appears from the outside, but as programmers we know that what is inside determines what the user sees; a program is a sequence of statements, both declarative and imperative, and each imperative statement can affect the state of the program. As programmers we should be able to understand how the program state is affected by executing each statement in sequence. This will, in fact, be our primary, though not exclusive, focus for the rest of these lessons. What we will learn through our investigation is that the semantics of a program can be seen as the *composition* of the changes to the state caused by the execution of each (imperative) program statement in its proper order.

Example 3 – Semantics for `AddThem`

▼

In Example 1 we introduced the notion of a specification for a program. The following is a C^{++} program which is supposed to implement the specification from that example. The program has been augmented with line numbers to help us keep track of the PC variable.

```
1    #include <iostream.h>

2    int main () {

3        float Sum;
4        int    Num1,
5               Num2;

6        cout << "Enter two (integer) values >> ";
7        cin >> Num1;
8        cin >> Num2;

9        Sum = Num1 + Num2;

10       cout << "The sum of the values is "
                << Sum << endl;
11   }
```

In this example we want to get a feel for how to link together the changes in state resulting from successive statements. Using our new definition of state, and assuming a representative set of input data, we can write down the initial state for the program as:

input stream:	$< v_1, v_2 >$
variables:	(Num1, no value)
	(Num2, no value)
	(Sum, no value)
PC:	6
output stream:	empty

and the final state for the program as:

input stream:	empty
variables:	(Num1, v_1)
	(Num2, v_2)
	(Sum, $< v_1 + v_2 >$)
PC:	11
output stream:	Enter two (real) values >>
	The sum of the values is $v1 + v2$

We have introduced a bit of new notation here. In particular, each identifier is represented by a pair, as required by the definition of program state. So in the initial state, each identifier is paired with "no value," which means that at that point we know nothing about what the paired value might be.

Continuing with the example, it is easy to see what happens to each component of the state as the program is executed one statement at a time. Here is the sequence of states which results from the execution of the program:

```
State

initial:   input stream:     < v₁, v₂ >
```
$< v_1, v_2 >$

```
           variables:        (Num1, no value)
                             (Num2, no value)
                             (Sum, no value)
           PC:               6
           output stream:    empty
```

```
6       cout << "Enter two (integer) values >> ";
```

```
        input stream:     < v₁, v₂ >
```
$< v_1, v_2 >$

```
        variables:        (Num1, no value)
                         (Num2, no value)
                         (Sum, no value)
        PC:               7
        output stream:    Enter two (real) values >>
```

```
7       cin >> Num1;
```

```
        input stream:     < v₂ >
```
$< v_2 >$

```
        variables:        (Num1, v₁)
```
$(\text{Num1}, v_1)$

```
                         (Num2, no value)
                         (Sum, no value)
        PC:               8
        output stream:    Enter two (real) values >>
```

```
8          cin >> Num2;
```

input stream: empty
variables: (Num1, v_1)
                 (Num2, v_2)
                 (Sum, no value)
PC: 9
output stream: Enter two (real) values >>

```
9          Sum = Num1 + Num2;
```

input stream: empty
variables: (Num1, v_1)
                 (Num2, v_2)
                 (Sum, $v_1 + v_2$)
PC: 10
output stream: Enter two (real) values >>

```
10         cout << "The sum of the values is "
                << Sum << endl;
```

State

final: input stream: empty
       variables: (Num1, v_1)
                        (Num2, v_2)
                        (Sum, $< v_1 + v_2 >$)
       PC: 11
       output stream: Enter two (real) values >>
                        The sum of the values is $v1 + v2$

It is important to notice how the state of the program changes as the program execution progresses. The way we link the initial state of the program with the final state of the program is by executing each statement in the environment created by the execution of the previous statement.

One interesting result of this example is that we actually have a demonstration that the program is correct. If we focus on the initial and final states and ignore the **variables** and PC parts of these, then we have the specification which appears in Example 1; i.e., the inherent semantics matches the intended semantics, and hence the program is correct. The intermediate states are just deduced from earlier states and our understanding of what the basic program statements do to the existing state.

▲

This is a lot of work just to understand one simple program! But, of course, we hope that the principles uncovered in this simple example will help us understand more complex programs for which the semantics may not be quite so obvious. What we can gain immediately from this example is the basic notion of the semantics of a program *statement*. If the semantics of a program is the change in program state caused by executing the program, then a similar definition should apply for statements, with "statement" substituted for "program." In fact, that is the definition we adopt.

Statement Semantics

The *semantics of a statement* is the change in the program state caused by the execution of the statement.

In the rest of our discussion of semantics it will be common for us to have to refer to the state of a program before or after a statement is executed. To allow for a smoother discussion we adopt the following definitions.

Pre-state of a Statement

The *pre-state* of a statement is the state of the program just *before* the statement is executed.

Post-state of a Statement

The *post-state* of a statement is the state of the program just *after* the statement is executed.

Lesson 3

Semantic Building Blocks

In these lessons we are not just interested in techniques for *writing* programs, but also in techniques for *understanding* and *explaining* programs, i.e., our rhetoric of programming. The idea is to develop a style of program writing which reflects in the text of the program our basic understanding of the semantics of the program. In the process of learning to program we want to build an intuition for determining from the text of a program what that program will accomplish when it is executed. In this and future lessons our goal will be to develop a persuasive style of programming which makes it easier to understand the programs we write. Of course, as a side effect you should end up writing better programs because of your increased awareness of semantics.

This lesson begins our detailed investigation of program semantics (from the programmer's perspective) by looking at the semantics of the declarative components of C^{++}. What we find in this lesson will set a context for our investigations of imperative semantics in the lessons to come. We will begin by looking at the basic building blocks of any (imperative) programming language, the declarative statements (i.e., identifier definitions) and expressions. We will end this lesson with an exploration of a technique for anticipating the possibility of computation errors during expression evaluation. Our interest will not be in preventing the computational errors, but in understanding in which program states the computational errors can occur.

This lesson assumes that you have been introduced to the following C^{++} concepts:

- simple data types
- identifier declarations
- arithmetic and Boolean expressions

3.1 Semantics of Declarative Statements

On page 15 in Lesson 2 we defined the *environment* of a program essentially to be the set of names used for objects in the program. We have also seen (Lesson 1.3) that the declarative statements in the program define this environment. In fact, each declarative statement causes one entry to be added to the environment. For this reason (i.e., that a change takes place in the environment), we will say that the semantics of a declarative statement is the addition to the environment of an entry for the identifier mentioned in the statement.

Of course, an environment entry does not consist solely of the identifier. Each declarative statement associates certain attributes with the identifier and it is these attributes which comprise the rest of an environment entry. In particular, we will define environment entries to have the following components:

1. identifier

2. data type

3. "flavor" (variable or constant)

4. initial value

Imperative languages (e.g., Pascal, C^{++}) can be divided into two groupings based on their treatment of declarative statements. Those in the Pascal camp require that declarative statements precede all imperative statements, while C^{++}-style languages allow declarative statements to occur anywhere that an imperative statement can occur. In this section we will look at both of these possibilities, but always in the C^{++} context.

Declaratives First

Two different kinds of declarative statements are of interest at this point: the variable declaration and constant declaration. The difference between these is a variable declaration permits but does not require an initial value to be given, while a constant declaration requires the initial value. Remember that when a program executes, every memory location has some initial value, so we will assume a default value "uninitialized" for those variable declarations where no initial value is specified (we will use "UI" as a short form for "uninitialized").

To see how the environment of a program grows, consider the following C^{++} program fragment:

```
#include <iostream.h>

int main () {
    const float Pi = 3.1415;

    int   Radius;
    float Area;

    int   NumCircles;
    float TotalArea;

    ...
}
```

What environment does this program fragment imply? First, remember that the environment is composed of entries, where each has an identifier, a type, a flavor, and a value. We want to write down the set of entries which comprise the environment.

The first line in the fragment is an include command. This is not really a C^{++} statement, but rather a command to the C^{++} compiler to include the text from the specified file, iostream.h, as part of the text of the program. This include file contains a sequence of declarative statements which define methods for accessing the input and output streams. From the include line we know that there will be entries for cin and cout. For a particular execution of the program we would be able to say what the input stream would be, but in this case we will just denote that by "input data." Before the program executes there is no way to know the status of the output stream, so the initial value associated with cout must be "UI." The environment first picks up an entry for each of these (externally) defined variable identifiers:

```
{(cin, character stream, V, "input data"),
 (cout, character stream, V, UI)}
```

The constant definition of Pi associates the value 3.1415 and the type float. We add this to the growing environment:

```
{(cin, character stream, V, "input data"),
 (cout, character stream, V, UI),
 (Pi, float, C, 3.1415)}
```

Finally, each of the variable declarations determines an entry including the identifier, the (explicitly) associated type, "V" since each is a variable, and the value "UI." With these entries added we have the program environment:

```
{(cin, character stream, V, "input data"),
 (cout, character stream, V, UI),
 (Pi, float, C, 3.1415), (Radius, int, V, UI),
 (Area, float, V, UI), (NumCircles, int, V, UI),
 (TotalArea, float, V, UI)}
```

This is quite straightforward. But, as indicated earlier, it is possible in C^{++} to have declarative statements intermixed among the imperative statements. Since this feature is a convenience rather than a necessity we will always place declarative statements at the beginning. For those interested, the following section discusses the impact of the more flexible placement of identifier definitions on the program environment.

Declaratives Anywhere (Optional)

Simple programs make it appear that the environment of a program, once established, is fixed. In fact, this is not true in two ways. First, the declarative statements don't have to occur all together at the beginning of the program. The following code is a legal C^{++} program.

```
#include <iostream.h>

int main () {

    int   Num1,
          Num2;

    cin >> Num1;
    cin >> Num2;

    float Sum;
    Sum = Num1 + Num2;

    cout << Sum << endl;
}
```

The environment for this program is not complete until the declaration of sum is encountered. Since sum is not referenced in the earlier statements of the program, the semantics of the program as a whole is not changed.

But there are other possibilities. A compound statement — a sequence of statements enclosed in curly braces — can occur anywhere in a C^{++} program. A compound statement establishes a new environment for the program containing it. When a declarative statement is encountered inside the compound statement, an entry is created as usual, but that entry is treated specially.

1. If the entry is for an identifier that is already in the program environment, then the new entry *shadows* the other entry. This means that the original entry is ignored, but not erased, while the new entry is in the environment.

2. When the enclosing brace is reached, any entry created in the compound statement is discarded. Notice that this means that entries which had been shadowed are now reinstated as visible members of the environment.

To see how the environment evolves in a program with a compound statement, consider the following C^{++} program:

```
#include <iostream.h>

1  int main () {

2      int   A, B, C;
3      float Disc;

4      cout << "Enter three integer coefficients > ";
5      cin >> A >> B >> C;

6      {
7          int Bsq, FourAC;
```

```
8          Bsq = B*B;
9          FourAC = 4*A*C;

10         disc = Bsq - FourAC;
11    }

12    cout << endl
           << "The discriminant = "
           << Disc << endl;
13 }
```

First, notice that since the identifiers declared in the compound statement are not already declared, no shadowing occurs in this example. The program environment is as follows:

As before, the environment first picks up entries for `cin`, `cout` from entries in the include file. We will assume that the input stream holds values as specified:

```
{(cin, character stream, V, "1 2 1"),
 (cout, character stream, V, UI)}
```

The declarations on lines 2 and 3 add four entries:

```
{(cin, character stream, V, "1 2 1"),
 (cout, character stream, V, "..."),
 (A, int, V, UI), (B, int, V, UI),
 (C, int, V, UI), (Disc, float, V, UI)}
```

When line 7 is reached, we enter a new local environment (which extends to line 11). The declaration on line 7 adds two new entries as follows:

```
{(cin, character stream, V, ""),
 (cout, character stream, V, "..."),
 (A, int, V, 1), (B, int, V, 2),
 (C, int, V, 1), (Disc, float, V, UI),
 (Bsq, int, V, UI), (FourAC, int, V, UI)}
```

When line 11 is finally reached, the environment entries created on line 7 are removed from the environment:

```
{(cin, character stream, V, ""),
 (cout, character stream, V, "..."),
 (A, int, V, 1), (B, int, V, 2),
 (C, int, V, 1), (Disc, float, V, 0.0)}
```

Finally, when line 13 is reached, the program terminates and the environment disappears.

3.2   Semantics of Expressions

We have seen that the declarative statements in a program establish an environment within which the program's imperative statements are executed. It is the impact of these imperative statements on the environment which underlies the semantics of a program. The most basic component of any imperative statement is the expression. When we see an expression in a program we think of it as being a value. But this is a result-oriented view – after the fact. On reflection we can see that an expression is actually a description of how to compute a value, or more simply, a description of a computation.

The expressions we usually think of, and are introduced to very early in our schooling, are arithmetic expressions. Here are a few examples of arithmetic expressions:

$$X$$
$$102$$
$$X + 5 * Y/10$$
$$(Z + Y) * (Z - (X - Y))$$

These expressions vary from the simple to the complex; in each case the expression represents a numeric value to be computed. But in programming there are other types of values which can be represented by expressions. The following examples are expressions representing character or Boolean values:

```
'A'
A + "some ending"
```
$$A \ \&\& \ B$$
$$! \ (A \ \&\& \ B)$$

Regardless of the types of values involved, these expressions all look reasonably familiar and we are intuitively aware of the computation described in each case. For example, in the expression ! $(A \ \&\& \ B)$, the values of A and B are combined via the "&&" operation to yield a new value which is then altered by the "!" operation.

When dealing with programming languages, however, intuitive understanding is not always sufficient. We need to know exactly what computation the computer will carry out no matter how complex the expression. Two important issues in this regard are

- the order in which operations are applied and

- the data type of the value which results when applying an operation to two operands.

Each language has rules which deal specifically with these issues. In C^{++} the order of operation is standard, with subexpressions in parentheses evaluated first and remaining operations applied in order of decreasing precedence (from left to right).[1] Determining the type of value which results from applying an operation to particular operands, on the other hand, varies from language to language. In C^{++} there is considerable flexibility for applying arithmetic operations, for example, to various types of operands. The important thing to remember for our purposes is that if a language allows a real value to be added to an integer value, there must be a rule which indicates what the type of the result will be. So, given any expression in C^{++} and a program state, it is possible to determine exactly what value will be computed and what its type is.

Given a particular program state, there are two important attributes of any expression: the *value* to be computed and the *type* of that computed value. For our purposes it is useful to combine these two attributes for an expression into a single "package" which we call the *semantic value* of the expression. (It will be our habit in future lessons to be casual about the use of the term *semantic value*, sometimes meaning just its value part and other times meaning both components. It should be clear from the context of the use which one is meant.)

Semantic Value

The *semantic value* of an expression in a given program state consists of the value computed for the expression in the given state and the type.

3.3 Identifying Computational Success

Our interest in semantic values relates to our desire to understand the semantics of imperative program statements. But in a particular state, if the evaluation of an expression results in a computational error (e.g., division by zero), then statement execution ceases and semantics becomes a non-issue. How do we prevent such failures from occurring? We will investigate this question in two parts: identify conditions that guarantee evaluation success, and then look at ways of guaranteeing that only those conditions can exist when evaluation occurs. We will deal with the first part now and save the second part for our discussion of the selection statement.

Example 4 – Computing a ratio
▼

> One sure way to get a program to fail is to include an expression which involves division by zero. The simplest form follows:
>
> X/Y

---

[1]This means, for example, that since multiplication has a higher precedence than addition, the expression $5 + 4 * 3$ describes the same computation as does the expression $5 + (4 * 3)$.

If the value of Y is zero when the evaluation is carried out, a hardware error results[2] – a clear computational failure. If, on the other hand, the value of Y is non-zero, then the evaluation is guaranteed to succeed. This is easy. The condition for computational success is *Y is not zero.*

But having discovered the condition, what should we do with it? First, the condition can be easily written in the form of a Boolean expression – Y != 0. We will see that writing the condition as a Boolean expression pays big dividends in later lessons. Now, if this expression appears in a program statement, we use the Boolean condition that we found as a comment for the program statement. Here's an example:

```
Result = X/Y;  // Require:  Y != 0
```

We call such a comment a `Require` clause since we would like to require that the condition be satisfied when the statement is executed. Of course, putting in the comment doesn't have any effect on the state, so the `Requirement` is really a reminder to the programmer to take action to ensure the condition will always be satisfied.

▲

Example 5 – Roots of a quadratic
▼

Given a quadratic equation $aX^2 + bX + c = 0$, we can write two expressions which describe its roots. We can incorporate the expressions into a program as follows:

```
root1 = (-b + sqrt(b*b - 4*a*c))/(2*a)
root2 = (-b - sqrt(b*b - 4*a*c))/(2*a)
```

We see right away that there is the possibility for division by zero, so the condition we want to guarantee is (a != 0). But also, each expression involves taking a square root, which we know will fail if the argument is negative. We can describe this second condition with the Boolean expression

```
(b*b - 4*a*c >= 0).
```

Since we require that both conditions be true (so that neither failure can occur) we must use the *conjunction* of the two; that is, join the two expressions with the AND operator. Similarly, the *disjunction* of two Boolean expressions is the OR of the two expressions.

---

[2]Division by zero can be detected by the computer hardware. When this situation is detected an internal error, called a *hardware error*, is generated; the operating system usually responds by terminating the program.

```
(a != 0)   AND   (b*b - 4*a*c >= 0)
```

The code can then be commented as follows:

```
// Require: (a != 0)   AND   (b*b - 4*a*c >= 0)
Root1 = (-b + sqrt(b*b - 4*a*c))/(2*a);
Root2 = (-b - sqrt(b*b - 4*a*c))/(2*a);
```

▲

    At this point, the expressions you will encounter will most likely fail for one of the two reasons illustrated above – dividing by zero or taking the root of a negative number. Later, when we encounter user-defined functions and the array data structure, we will see that expression failure can depend on other factors as well. For now, given an expression, we want to be able to write down the condition that must be met in order for the expression to yield a result – i.e., if the program state satisfies the condition, then the expression will yield a value.

    This technique of supplying a `Require` clause with expressions which can fail is the first rhetorical technique we have developed. Notice that the purpose of the clause is to remind the programmer what the program should do; the clause does not indicate what the program actually does. That will be the responsibility of our next rhetorical technique to be introduced in the next lesson. At this point it is important to remember that consistency of style is crucial; be sure that you appropriately comment *all* expressions which can fail.

3.4 A Bit More Formally – Expression Satisfaction

In the previous section we saw the use of a comment containing a Boolean expression to specify a condition on the state of the program. The idea was for the programmer, through the use of appropriate program statements, to ensure that the program state satisfies the condition at that particular point in the program. Since this use of Boolean expressions will be the main tool employed in the following lessons, it will be useful to look at the idea in a bit more detail. There are two main points to examine. First, what does it mean for a program state to satisfy an expression? Second, what is a Boolean expression really supposed to reflect about program state?

Satisfaction

A Boolean expression is one that will always give one of two results: `true` or `false`. We evaluate a Boolean expression in a particular program state by first replacing each variable name in the expression with its value in the state and then carrying out the computation specified by the new expression (resulting from the substitutions). If the resulting value is `true` then we say that the state satisfies the expression.

Satisfies

A program state *satisfies* a Boolean expression if the expression obtained by substituting each identifier in the expression by its value in the state evaluates to `true`.

This notion of satisfaction is fairly simple, but, as we will see in the remaining lessons, it plays a central role in our ability to express program semantics.

Example 6 – Satisfaction
▼

Suppose we have a program whose current state is

```
{(a,int,4), (b,int,5), (c,int,6),
 (Root,real,0.0), (Done,bool,false)}
```

Based on this state we can check the following expressions and their evaluations. The table shows the original expression, its substituted form, the computed result, and whether in the specified state the expression is satisfied.

expression	substitution	value	satisfied?
a > b	4 > 5	false	no
a != 0	4 != 0	true	yes
true	true	true	yes
b*b – 4*a*c >= 0	5*5 – 4*4*6 >= 0	false	no
b > a AND Done	5 > 4 AND false	false	no
b > a OR Done	5 > 4 OR false	true	yes

One thing to point out in this sequence of evaluations is that if a particular variable name does not appear in an expression, then the expression's final value is independent of the variable's value. In particular, the expression `true` is one which is satisfied in every state for every program.

▲

The Weak and the Strong

Now for the second question: What is a Boolean expression supposed to reflect about the state of a program? Let's return to Example 4 in which the following line of code is discussed:

```
Result = X/Y;  // Require:  Y != 0
```

The `Require` clause is supposed to give a condition which guarantees the expression X/Y will evaluate without error. In terms of satisfaction this means that the expression X/Y will evaluate without error if the program state *satisfies* the `Require` clause.

It is useful to think of the Boolean expression in a `Require` clause as defining a set of states which satisfy the Boolean expression. In this way, when the program execution reaches the clause, the state of the program should be in that set described by the `Require` clause. This introduces an interesting question. In the example above, what is so special about the Boolean expression (Y != 0)? Why not comment the code as follows?

```
Result = X/Y;  // Require:  Y > 0
```

Or, for that matter, why not the following?

```
Result = X/Y;  // Require:  Y < 0
```

In either of these cases, if the state satisfies the specified `Require` clause then no error can occur. Of course, we intuitively know the answer: if we use one of the alternative clauses then there can be program states which don't satisfy the clause but don't cause an error. These two alternative clauses seem to filter out program states which are, in fact, acceptable.

We can describe this situation more formally. If we have two Boolean expressions A and B, then we say that A is *weaker* than B if the set of states defined by B is a subset of the set of states defined by A. Notice that Y != 0 is weaker than both Y > 0 and Y < 0. Not surprisingly, we also say, in this situation, that B is *stronger* than A. So if we have an expression such as (Y > 0) which filters out too many states, then we want to find a weaker expression (we want to weaken the expression).

When looking for a suitable `Require` clause we want to find an expression which is weak, but not too weak. Remember that weakness means letting in lots of states, so "not too weak" means not letting in too many states. There are situations where finding the weakest expressions involves reducing the number of permitted states. Consider the following two expressions:

```
A:  a > 0
B:  b*b - 4*a*c
```

which naturally occur in Example 5. We can see that each one separately is too weak to act as a `Require` clause for the code in that example – i.e., there are states which satisfy A and not B and *vice versa*. The way to get the expression we need is to take the conjunction (AND) of A and B. This effectively strengthens each expression, resulting in the Boolean expression appropriate for the `Require` clause in the example. (Notice that the AND operation coincides with taking the intersection of the two sets of satisfying states.)

Lesson 4

Semantics of
Simple Statements

To this point we have been setting the stage for the discussion of semantics and persuasive programming. Remember that the idea is to develop a strategy or style of programming which is *persuasive*; we will take this to mean that a reading of a completed program will persuade the reader that the program is correct. This, of course, begs the question: What is meant by "persuade?" The answer will emerge as we look at the semantics of the various program statements of C^{++}. For each statement we will describe a method for recording its semantics in the form of a program comment known as an *assertion*. A program, then, will consist of sequences of program statements and assertions. It is the sequence of assertions which will form the persuasive argument for the program's correctness.

We will begin this lesson by defining the notion of assertion. Then we will discuss the semantics of the simple C^{++} statements, show how assertions can be used to explain the semantics of these statements, and discuss strategies for placing assertions in sequences of program code.

This lesson requires the same familiarity with C^{++} as for the preceding lessons.

4.1   Assertions

We have been given a program specification and have written a program which we believe meets the specification. How can we convince someone else (or ourselves, for that matter) that the program does what it is supposed to do – i.e., that the program meets its specification? We have basically two choices:

1. Generate an exhaustive set of test data and show that the program performs as specified on each data set.

2. Give a general argument (independent of specific data values) that the program state will change as specified.

For most programs the number of possible data sets is too large to make the first approach practical. The second approach, however, holds more promise. If we understand how program statements change the program state (i.e., their semantics), then we should be able to determine how sequences of statements change the state and consequently how the whole program changes the initial state to the final state.

Our approach will be to borrow the Boolean expression idea from the `Require` clause of the last lesson, and apply it to describe state change. The following code sequence reflects this idea:

```
// A:  X has a value AND Y > 0
Z = X + Y;
// B:  Z == X + Y AND Z > X
```

The Boolean expression labelled `A` in the first comment reflects what the programmer knows to be true before the statement is to be executed: the variables `X` and `Y` have values and the value of `Y` is positive. The expression labelled `B` in the second comment indicates state information (that the new value of `Z` is the same as the value of `X+Y`) and also a conclusion based on the first comment, namely, that the value of `Z` must exceed the value of `X`. The expression in the comments before and after the statement reflect not just the (specific) state of the program at that point, but also relationships among the values for the variables `X`, `Y` and `Z`. The Boolean expressions in the comments are called *assertions*, though we will often abuse the notation and use the term *assertion* to refer to the comment itself.

Assertion

An *assertion* is a Boolean expression which is true for the state of the program at a particular point in the program.

Assertions state relationships among values of variables in the program environment. In writing assertions we make use of the six comparison operators our programming language gives us (e.g., > (greater than), >= (greater than or equal), < (greater than), <= (less than or equal), == (equal), and != (not equal)) as well as the usual Boolean operations (AND, OR, NOT).[1]

We will use assertions in two ways in programming. Isolated assertions will be used to reflect what we know about the state of the program at a particular point, usually between two statements. Assertions will also be used in pairs,

---

[1]We use AND, OR, and NOT rather than the corresponding C^{++} operators, '&&', '||', and '!', in an attempt to differentiate assertions from program expressions.

where the first assertion reflects the status of the program before a statement is executed and the second assertion reflects the status after the statement is executed. When used in this way we will refer to them as the statement's *precondition* and *postcondition*.

There are two basic ways to represent assertions in a program. Some languages have a built-in function, usually called `assert`, which takes a Boolean expression (the assertion) as its parameter. The program executes the `assert` function and halts if the argument evaluates to `false` – an error message is printed. The way we will represent assertions in this text (and we encourage you to use them in your programming) is in the form of a comment, as has been illustrated already. All assertion comments will have the form

```
// Assert: ......
```

Programs that include assertions are said to be *asserted*. Using our form of assertion, the previous segment of code would be more properly asserted as follows:

```
// Assert: X has a value AND Y > 0
Z = X + Y;
// Assert: Z == X + Y AND Z > X
```

4.2 Semantics of Assignment

The assignment statement is one of three mechanisms used in C^{++}, and in most imperative programming langauges, for changing the state of a program, the others being the input statement and the function call with reference parameter(s).

The syntax for the assignment statement is very simple and is illustrated by the following example:

```
disc = b*b - 4*a*c;
```

There are two components separated by the assignment operator "=" — a variable name on the left-hand side and an expression on the right-hand side.

Informally, we know the assignment statement as an instruction that computes the value for an expression (the right-hand side) and stores the resulting value in a variable (the left-hand side). More formally, we can say that the *semantic value* of the expression is stored in the variable named on the left (if the types of the two sides are the same!). In the exceptional cases, where the variable and the expression have different types, the value of the expression must be converted to an appropriate (equivalent) value of the identifier's type before the (converted) value is stored. The following statement puts these ideas in the language of semantics:

- If the types associated with `<identifier>` and `<expression>` are the same, the semantic value of `<identifier>` in the post-state is the semantic value of `<expression>` in the pre-state.

- If the type associated with `<identifier>` is different from the type associated with `<expression>`, then the semantic value of `<identifier>` in the post-state is determined by converting the semantic value of `<expression>` in the pre-state to an "appropriate" semantic value of `<identifier>`'s type.

The basic semantics of the assignment statement was illustrated in Example 3 at statement 7. The pre- and post-states for that statement are repeated here.

```
input stream:    empty
variables:       (Num1, v₁)
                 (Num2, v₂)
                 (Sum, UI)
PC:              7
output stream:   Enter two (real) values >>
```

$$7 \quad \text{Sum} = \text{Num1} + \text{Num2};$$

```
input stream:    empty
variables:       (Num1, v₁)
                 (Num2, v₂)
                 (Sum, v₁ + v₂)
PC:              8
output stream:   Enter two (real) values >>
```

Notice that before the statement is executed Sum is uninitialized and after it is executed it has value $v_1 + v_2$, the value computed for the expression "Num1 + Num2."

One subtle point must be emphasized. When the semantic value of the expression is determined, it must be based on the *pre*-state of the statement. This is important because it is possible for the identifier that appears on the left to also appear as a component of the expression on the right.

Example 7 – Incrementing a variable (I)
▼

Consider the following problem for which we are to complete the post-state:

```
{ (Score, v₁), (Fudge, v₂) }
Score = Score * Fudge;
{ (Score, ?), (Fudge, ?)  }
```

The semantics of the assignment statement says we compute the semantic value for the expression on the right in the pre-state. So the expression evaluates to $v_1 * v_2$, using v_1 as the value of Score and v_2 as the value of Fudge. This semantic value becomes the value of `Score` in the post-state; the value of `Fudge` doesn't change. We have the following result:

```
{ (Score, v₁), (Fudge, v₂) }
Score = Score * Fudge;
{ (Score, v₁ * v₂), (Fudge, v₂) }
```

▲

4.3   Asserting the Assignment Statement

While the semantics of the assignment statement is quite intuitive, it is important to take a careful look at how we represent that semantics in terms of assertions. We will find that there are principles that we can adopt and also certain situations to watch out for.

To begin we can look at the following simple assignment statement. We want to first write as complete a postcondition as possible and then see how we can reasonably simplify that postcondition:

```
// Assert: X, Y have values
X = Y + 5;
// Assert: ???
```

What statement can we make about the state of the program after the assignment is executed? There are two things: the value of Y remains unchanged and the value of X becomes the value of Y (in the pre-state) plus 5. From this detailed description we learn that in the postcondition we must be able to refer to both the value Y had in the pre-state and the value Y has in the post-state. We adopt the practice of appending "(pre)" to the beginning of a variable name in order to refer to the variable's value in the pre-state. Based on this new notation we can assert the assignment statement as follows:

```
// Assert: X, Y have values
X = Y + 5;
// Assert: Y == (pre)Y AND
//         X == (pre)Y + 5
```

Now we have come to this postcondition by following the definition of assignment semantics and applying the new notation – but it seems a bit complex for the situation. Is there any way we can simplify what we have? The answer, not surprisingly, is yes. We will refer to any condition of the form "Y == (pre)Y" as the *identity condition*[2] on, in this case, Y. This condition says that in the postcondition Y can replace (pre)Y, since their values are the same. So we get the following simplified postcondition:

---

[2]We will also call the condition "(pre)Y == Y" the identify condition on Y.

```
// Assert: X, Y have values
X = Y + 5;
// Assert: Y == (pre)Y AND
//           X == Y + 5
```

One final point can be learned from this example. While writing down the identity condition for Y was useful for coming up with the simplified postcondition, the fact that Y doesn't change is pretty obvious. If there were more variables involved in the expression it would still be only X whose value would change. So we will adopt the rule that when writing a postcondition, suppress all identity conditions in the final asserted form. This practice will help highlight the conditions which *do* reflect change in the state.

Persuasive Principle 1

Suppress all identity conditions in final asserted forms.

Following this principle, then, we arrive at the following final asserted form for our assignment statement:

```
// Assert: X, Y have values
X = Y + 5;
// Assert: X == Y + 5
```

Example 8 – Incrementing a variable (II)
▼

The example we looked at above has the nice characteristic that the value of X can be described making reference only to values in the post-state of the assignment. But what happens in the following assignment statement?

```
// Assert: Sum has a value
Sum = Sum + Num;
// Assert: ???
```

We proceed as in the previous example by first giving a complete assertion for the assignment:

```
// Assert: Sum has a value
Sum = Sum + Num;
// Assert: Num == (pre)Num AND
//           Sum == (pre)Sum + (pre)Num
```

Remember that the condition for Sum has the specified form because its new value is computed in the pre-state. But now we simplify using the identity condition for Num and imposing the first persuasive principle.

```
// Assert: Sum has a value
Sum = Sum + Num;
// Assert: Sum == (pre)Sum + Num
```

Notice that, while this is almost as simple as the previous example, here we cannot get rid of the reference to (pre)Sum. This is because the new value of Sum depends on the previous value of Sum. We can simplify no more.

▲

From these two examples we find that eliminating references to (pre) makes assertions correspond better to our intuition, but it is not always possible to eliminate all such references. We will adopt the following second persuasive principle.

Persuasive Principle 2

When writing postconditions eliminate references to (pre) whenever possible.

4.4 Being Persuasive

Persuasive programming is more than simply representing the semantics of isolated program statements; it is using the semantics of program statements to determine properties of the state at various points in a program. It is often the case that the exact value of a variable at a particular point in a program is of less interest than how the variable's value relates to some other value. For example, if the fact that the variable X is guaranteed to be positive is important, we might choose the asserted segment on the left rather than that on the right:

```
// Assert: X has a value        // Assert: X has a value
X = X*X + 1;                     X = X*X + 1;
// Assert: X > 0                 // Assert: X ==
                                 //           (pre)X*(pre)X + 1
```

In a similar vein, the precondition of a statement may specify a more complex relationship among variables and values. Consider the following segment, for example:

```
// Assert: X > 0 AND Y >= 0
Y = Y + X;
// Assert: ???
```

If it is the relative values of X and Y which are important then we might supply the following postcondition:

```
// Assert: X > 0 AND Y >= 0
Y = Y + X;
// Assert: X > 0 AND Y > 0
```

The fact that Y is positive in the post-state is a consequence of the precondition and the semantics of the assignment statement: if X is positive and Y is positive or zero, then the value of Y+X will always be positive.

These examples illustrate that there are two kinds of expressions used in assertions: those that specify that a variable has a particular value and those that specify that variables satisfy certain other relationships. It is important when programming to be aware of which type of assertion is appropriate (possibly both).

4.5   Semantics of I/O Statements

We have already discussed the importance of input and output to our understanding of the semantics of a program. But, as has been the case with expressions and the assignment statement, there is more to the input and output statements than might meet the eye. In C^{++} the common mechanisms for standard input and output (keyboard input and screen output) are the stream identifiers cin and cout and the extraction ($>>$) and insertion ($<<$) operators.

Output

Since our main interest is the programmer's rather than the user's view of a program, we are primarily interested in how statements alter the strictly internal environment of a program. Since changes to the output stream are only observable by the user, we will tend to ignore the impact of an output statement on the program environment.

Input

As is the case for all program statements, the semantics of an input statement is the change its execution causes in the program state. The only parts of the state that can change are the variable arguments to the statement and the input stream. For the variable arguments, the input statements are just special purpose assignment statements: an argument to cin, which must be a variable, is treated as the left-hand side of an assignment, and the next value in the input stream is treated as the value of the expression on the right-hand side.

Since the variable arguments to the input statements can be of the types `int`, `float`, or `char`, you might conclude that the input stream is a heterogeneous sequence of data values. In fact, the input stream is a sequence of character values. The data typed at the keyboard comes to a program in character form, rather than in the form of the values to be assigned to the variable arguments. This means that if there is a variable parameter of type `int`, then the sequence of typed characters must be converted to a proper integer form (i.e., binary representation) before the value is stored as the value of the variable.

Part II

Statement Semantics:
A First Look

Lesson 5

Semantics and High-Level Statements

Part I of this text has described the two basic characteristics of programming languages: syntax and semantics. Most of the discussion has centered on semantics, and we ended with an analysis of the semantics of the simple C^{++} program statements: assignment, input, and output. In addition to these simple statements there are four traditional ways of combining program statements into high-level control structures:

- *sequencing*
- *abstraction*
- *selection*
- *repetition*

In each of the next four lessons we will look at one of these high-level structures in the light of persuasive programming. Part II of this text carries forward the study of semantics to include these high-level control structures.

This second part of the text is designed to be a bit more flexible. It is important to read this lesson first, but the remaining three lessons can be read in any order. In the current lesson we will first look at the semantics of sequencing; then we will discuss how assertions are used in the remaining lessons of Part II.

5.1   The Semantics of Statement Sequences

The most basic of the high-level control structures is statement sequencing – known as *sequential control*. While the other control structures have complex syntax to signal their presence, statement sequences are represented simply by the normal layout of text – the sequence is indicated by placing statements one after the other in the intended order of execution.

In addition to normal statement sequencing, C^{++} has a control structure called the *compound statement*, which is an abstraction of sequential control – its simple syntax has the sequence of statements enclosed by matching curly braces. This structure is provided for two purposes:

1. to syntactically single out a specific statement sequence and

2. to provide a mechanism for introducing nested scope.

In fact we have seen this type of statement already as the body of the `main` function of a program – see, for example, the code on page 10.

Before looking in detail at the semantics of sequential control we will review some general principles from Part I. Let us suppose that S is some C^{++} statement – we are not saying if it is simple or high-level. By the semantics of S we mean the change in the program state which results from the execution of S. We have chosen to represent the semantics of S through the use of assertions as pre- and postconditions, as follows:

```
// Assert: Spre
S;
// Assert: Spost
```

Our goal, as implied in the previous lesson, is that `Spost` should reference values in the post-state of S and only reference values in the pre-state of S when necessary (Persuasive Principle 1). We have also adopted the practice of suppressing identity conditions for any variables in the environment whose values don't change as a result of executing S (Persuasive Principle 2).

Keeping these ideas and principles in mind, how can we come to an understanding of the semantics of a sequence? We will start by analyzing the following example:

```
// Assert: X, Y, Z have values
Y = X + 3;
Z = Y * (X + 1);
// Assert: ???
```

We want to complete the postcondition, but it seems that to be sure of our result we should analyze both of the statements separately. Applying what we learned in the previous lesson, we can generate the following asserted segments: the left column results from analyzing the first assignment statement; the right column from analyzing the second assignment in light of the left column. Also notice that, in moving from left to right, the fact that X doesn't change is used to simplify the first assignment's postcondition, in accordance with Persuasive Principle 2.

```
// Assert: X, Y, Z          // Assert: X, Y, Z
//           have values    //           have values
Y = X + 3;                  Y = X + 3;
// Assert: Y == (pre)X+3    // Assert: Y == X+3
```

```
Z = Y * (X + 1);              Z = Y * (X + 1);
// Assert: ???                // Assert: Z ==
                             //         (pre)Y*((pre)X+1)
                             //         AND
                             //         (pre)Y == (pre)X+3
```

The right column code relies on the observation that the postcondition for the first assignment becomes the precondition for the second assignment. Also remember that the condition stated in the second assertion can be carried forward to the postcondition if we remember that we must add (pre)s to make it relative to the pre-state. Joining the two conditions by AND is clearly appropriate because both conditions are true in the post-state. Now, making use of the fact that neither Y nor X changed in the second assignment, we can replace (pre)X with X and (pre)Y with X+3, giving the following:

```
// Assert: X, Y, Z have values
Y = X + 3;
// Assert: Y == X+3
Z = Y * (X + 1);
// Assert: Z == (X+3)*(X+1) AND
//          Y == X+3
```

Since the information contained in the second assertion has been factored into the new postcondition, we can eliminate the middle assertion altogether. Our sequence, then, has the following asserted form:

```
// Assert: X, Y, Z have values
Y = X + 3;
Z = Y * (X + 1);
// Assert: Z == (X+3)(X+1) AND
//          Y == X+3
```

One thing that made this example relatively easy is the fact that each postcondition could be written in terms of post-state values – i.e., we didn't have to use (pre). Determining the sequence's postcondition was a simple matter of using the equality in the first postcondition to help determine the second postcondition. Clearly, if our sequence consisted of three assignment statements, then the procedure could be carried one step further.

Example 9 – Asserting a sequence (I)
▼

Consider the following sequence of three assignment statements. We want to write an appropriate postcondition for it:

```
// Assert: X, Y, Z have values
Y = X + 3;
Z = X * 4;
X = Y + Z;
// Assert: ???
```

The first two assignment statements can be analyzed in the same way as the first example above. It is an exercise to fill in the details leading to the following:

```
// Assert: X, Y, Z have values
Y = X + 3;
Z = X * 4;
// Assert: Y == X+3 AND Z == X*4
X = Y + Z;
```

The next step takes a bit more care. We will do the details just as we did in the first example above. If we write out the natural postcondition for the third assignment we get the following:

```
// Assert: X, Y, Z have values
Y = X + 3;
Z = X * 4;
// Assert: Y == X+3 AND Z == X*4
X = Y + Z;
// Assert: X == (pre)Y + (pre)Z
```

Now we can bring forward the condition in the middle assertion, being sure to add (pre)s:

```
// Assert: X, Y, Z have values
Y = X + 3;
Z = X * 4;
// Assert: Y == X+3 AND Z == X*4
X = Y + Z;
// Assert: X == (pre)Y + (pre)Z
//         (pre)Y == (pre)X+3
//         (pre)Z == (pre)X*4
```

Since Y and Z do not change in the final assignment, we can replace the (pre)Ys and (pre)Zs by Y and Z, respectively. But this cannot be said for the variable X, since it appears on the left-hand side of the assignment. By doing the appropriate substitutions for Y and Z, we get our final asserted form.

```
// Assert: X, Y, Z have values
Y = X + 3;
Z = X * 4;
X = Y + Z;
// Assert: X == ((pre)X+3) + ((pre)X*4)
//         Y == (pre)X+3
//         Z == (pre)X*4
```

▲

The previous example brings up an important question. The postcondition for the sequence contains (pre)X. But to what does (pre)X refer? The immediate reaction is to say it refers to the value of X in the pre-state, but how do we interpret that – pre-state of the last assignment or pre-state of the sequence? Happily in this case the answer is "both." The value of X doesn't change in the first two assignments, so the value of X is the same in the sequence's pre-state and in the last assignment's pre-state. That answer, in a sense, avoids the question – it doesn't give us any guidance for other more complex situations.

Example 10 – Asserting a sequence (II)
▼

Consider the following sequence of two assignment statements for which we want to write an appropriate postcondition:

```
// Assert: X, Z have values
X = X + 3;
Z = X + Z;
// Assert: ???
```

This looks a bit tricky because the new value of each variable is defined in terms of its original value, but the analysis will lead to an important principle. The first step is straightforward and based on the work we did in the last lesson. The first assignment's postcondition can be written as follows:

```
// Assert: X, Z have values
X = X + 3;
// Assert: X == (pre)X+3
Z = X + Z;
// Assert: ???
```

Now for the second statement. We see that the value of Z depends on the values of both X and Z in the pre-state. Here is the obvious postcondition:

```
// Assert: X, Z have values
X = X + 3;
// Assert: X == (pre)X+3
Z = X * Z;
// Assert: Z == (pre)X * (pre)Z
```

But in this situation we are not really interested in the semantics of the individual assignment statements; we are interested in the cumulative effect of both assignments in sequence. We would like to eliminate the middle assertion so that the resulting pre- and postconditions reflect the semantics of the two assignments in sequence – i.e., as though they comprised a single statement.

Focusing on X for a moment, when we look at the assertion

```
// Assert: Z == (pre)X * (pre)Z
```

we know that `(pre)X` refers to the value of X after the first assignment. It would seem that, factoring in the new value of X from the first assignment, and the fact that the value of Z doesn't change, we should write the final assertion as

```
// Assert: Z == ((pre)(pre)X + 3) * (pre)(pre)Z
```

And if we use this assertion as our postcondition then the middle assertion is no longer needed. Notice that the complex form `(pre)(pre)` refers to the state two statements ago.

```
// Assert: X, Z have values
X = X + 3;
Z = X * Z;
// Assert: Z == ((pre)(pre)X + 3) * (pre)(pre)Z
```

▲

The result of this last example is a bit unsettling. It carries the specter of long sequences of (pre)s strung together – not a pretty picture. But we should return to our primary interest here – not the semantics of individual statements, but rather the semantics of sequences of statements. We want to treat a sequence as though it were a unit. With this in mind, it would seem reasonable to assert the example's code segment as follows:

```
// Assert: X, Z have values
X = X + 3;
Z = X * Z;
// Assert: Z == ((pre)X + 3) * (pre)Z
```

where the (pre)s are interpreted to refer to the state before the execution of the sequence of statements. In the next example we apply this idea to a longer sequence of statements.

Example 11 – Asserting a sequence (III)
▼

Assert the following sequence.

```
// Assert: X, Y, Z have values
X = X + 3;
Y = Y + 4;
X = X * Y;
Z = Z + X;
// Assert: ???
```

The first two statements are easy to handle. The left and right columns below reflect the first two steps of the analysis:

```
// Assert: X, Y, Z            // Assert: X, Y, Z
//            have values      //            have values
X = X + 3;                     X = X + 3;
// Assert: X == (pre)X+3
Y = Y + 4;                     Y = Y + 4;
                               // Assert: Y == (pre)Y + 4
                               //            AND
                               //            X == (pre)X + 3
X = X * Y;                     X = X * Y;
Z = Z + X;                     Z = Z + X;
// Assert: ???
```

Remember that both occurrences of (pre) in the right column refer to values in the pre-state of the first assignment.

> **Note:** We can think of this process as starting with the precondition and *pulling* that condition through the first assignment and then through the second. As a condition is pulled through a statement it accumulates more restrictions. It might be better to think of pulling a *copy* of the precondition so that it is clear that the precondition remains in place at the beginning of the sequence to act as an anchor for references to (pre).

We continue this process by pulling the new assertion through the third assignment. This happens in two steps. When it is pulled through we leave the original and produce the new assertion by applying the assignment semantics.

```
// Assert: X, Y, Z
//            have values      <=== anchor
X = X + 3;
Y = Y + 4;
// Assert: Y == (pre)Y + 4  <=== assignment precondition
//            AND
//            X == (pre)X + 3
X = X * Y;
// Assert: X ==
//            (pre)X * (pre)Y <=== new
Z = Z + X;
// Assert: ???
```

Now we must resolve the (pre)s and remove the "assignment precondition." Both (pre)s in the "new" assertion refer to the state before the assignment statement. In order to eliminate the "assignment precondition" two substitutions must be made, one for `(pre)X` and one for `(pre)Y`.

1. `(pre)X` in the "new" assertion refers to the value of X in the pre-state – the "original" assertion indicates this to be the value `(pre)X+3`, where the `(pre)X` is the value at the anchor. So we substitute `(pre)X+3` for `(pre)X`, knowing that the new `(pre)X` still refers to the value at the precondition.

2. Since Y doesn't change when the third assignment is executed, Y and `(pre)Y` are the same. So `(pre)Y+4` is substituted for `(pre)Y`. The new `(pre)Y` still refers to the value at the anchor.

These substitutions leave us with the following asserted form:

```
// Assert: X, Y, Z have values        <=== anchor
X = X + 3;
Y = Y + 4;
X = X * Y;
// Assert: X == ((pre)X + 3) * ((pre)Y + 4) AND
//            Y == (pre)Y + 4
Z = Z + X;
// Assert: ???
```

Now for the final pull. This time we can see that the values of X and Y do not change, but the value of Z does. Again we work in stages. First pull the just-completed assertion through the final assignment statement.

```
// Assert: X, Y, Z have values
X = X + 3;
Y = Y + 4;
X = X * Y;
// Assert: X == ((pre)X + 3) * ((pre)Y + 4) AND
//            Y == (pre)Y + 4
Z = Z + X;
// Assert: Z == (pre)Z + (pre)X
```

Since this is the first time the value of Z has changed, the value of `(pre)Z` is the same as for the original precondition. Also, since the values of X and Y are unchanged by the assignment, their `(pre)` references can be brought through unaltered. So we can eliminate the assignment precondition once its information is factored into the postcondition. The process yields the following final asserted form:

```
// Assert: X, Y, Z have values
X = X + 3;
Y = Y + 4;
X = X * Y;
Z = Z + X;
// Assert: Z == (pre)Z +
//                  ( ((pre)X + 3) * ((pre)Y + 4) )
//          AND
//          X == ((pre)X + 3) * ((pre)Y + 4)
//          AND
//          Y == (pre)Y + 4
```

▲

In each of the preceding examples the use of (**pre**) gives a rather abstract flavor to the postconditions. Though this is unavoidable in general, we can make things more palatable by considering the following modified version of the last example's code:

```
// Assert: input stream == <v1, v2, v3>
cin >> X >> Y >> Z;

X = X + 3;
Y = Y + 4;
X = X * Y;
Z = Z + X;
// Assert: Z == (pre)Z + ( ((pre)X + 3) * ((pre)Y + 4) ) AND
//          X == ((pre)X + 3) * ((pre)Y + 4)            AND
//          Y == (pre)Y + 4
```

Now, we can link each occurrence of (**pre**) with an actual value from the input. The postcondition can now be written as follows:

```
// Assert: input stream == <v1, v2, v3>
cin >> X >> Y >> Z;

X = X + 3;
Y = Y + 4;
X = X * Y;
Z = Z + X;
// Assert: Z == v3 + ( (v1 + 3) * (v2 + 4) ) AND
//          X == (v1 + 3) * (v2 + 4)         AND
//          Y == v2 + 4
```

5.2   Being More General

The examples of the previous section illustrate of a particular pattern of analysis which should go on whenever a sequence of statements is to be asserted.

Consider a code segment patterned as follows:

```
// Assert: Pre
S1;
S2;
...
Sn;
```

When we set about to determine the semantics of this sequence we first assume that the sequence should be treated as a high-level statement – i.e., we should determine a postcondition to follow `Sn` in which any reference to (`pre`) refers back to the program state before `S1`. The analytical process of finding the postcondition hinges on the notion of *pulling* a condition through a statement. There are three aspects to this pulling process:

1. Determine a postcondition for the statement through which the condition is pulled.

2. Incorporate into the postcondition the precondition, with all variable references replaced by their (`pre`) versions.

3. Simplify the resulting postcondition.

Except for the first statement, when a precondition is pulled through a statement, the precondition is removed from the code. This is reasonable since the content of the condition has been incorporated into the postcondition in step 2. The following sequences illustrate the steps:

```
// Pre     // Pre     // Pre     // Pre     // Pre          // Pre
S1;        S1;        S1;        S1;        S1;             S1;
S2;        // post1   S2;        S2;        S2;             S2;
S3;        S2;        // post2   S3;        S3;             S3;
...        S3;        S3;        // post3  ...             ...
Sn;        ...        ...        ...        // post(n-1)    Sn;
           Sn;        Sn;        Sn;        Sn;             // Post
```

The sequence precondition acts as an anchor for the pulling process and, as indicated earlier, marks the sequence pre-state to which all references to (`pre`) in the postcondition refer. The result is that from a semantic point of view the sequence of statements appears as a single high-level statement, with the pre- and postconditions giving its semantics. The important connection between references to (`pre`) in the high-level statement's precondition and the statement's pre-state is summarized in the third of our principles of persuasive programming:

Persuasive Principle 3

When `(pre)X` appears in the postcondition of a high-level statement it always refers to the value of `X` in the pre-state of the statement.

5.3   Reflecting on Assertions

In this lesson and the lessons to come you are encouraged to use assertions to reflect the semantics of statements in your programs. So far the motivation for this approach has been the classic, somewhat academic, "because it's there" – programming langauges have both syntactic and semantic aspects, so it is important to study and use both when writing programs. While this is a fine reason for pursuing persuasive programming, the reader may want a more practical rationale for the pursuit.

Why Use Assertions?

While the use of assertions is not a requirement in programming, there are very good reasons to adopt a programming style that includes their use. First, it is easy for students learning to program to be distracted by the syntactic side of a language – when an error occurs they look at the syntax of what they have written, rather than thinking about the meaning (semantics) of what they have written. The use of assertions helps to focus a student's attention on the semantic side.

Because the use of assertions helps focus attention on semantics, their continued use helps to build semantic intuition, and it is semantic intuition which is so important for effective programming.

Finally, the use of assertions in the more formal context of persuasive programming provides a strong intuitive base from which to learn more formal approaches to semantics.

How Do We Use Assertions?

In this text we use assertions in three different but related ways. First, we use assertions to describe the general semantics of the various programming statements. We do so by deriving, from a precondition and our intuitive understanding of a statement, a postcondition for the statement. This general semantic description provides a strategy for determining how to assert a particular statement in a program.

Second, we use assertions as a tool for analyzing the semantics of segments of code. One of the more difficult aspects of programming is the lack of analytical tools which can be used to expose semantic errors in code. Starting with an understanding of statement semantics assertions can help to analyze the semantics of specific program statements.

The third way we use assertions is in persuasive programming. Persuasive programming, in a sense, is the end result of combining assertion-based statement semantics with assertion-based semantic analysis. This approach will be used throughout the remainder of the text.

Approaches To Programming Persuasively

Our original rationale for learning persuasive programming was to facilitate the writing of persuasive programs, i.e., programs which contain evidence of their own correctness. So far we have talked about what persuasive programming is supposed to produce, but not how it is to be carried out. We can identify three basic approaches to doing persuasive programming, and they characterize three different levels of programming sophistication.

Assert After

> The first approach is to take an already written code segment and add assertions to reflect the segment's semantics. In this method you usually start with a precondition and progress through the segment deducing each subsequent assertion. In the end you should have a postcondition for the code segment, which means you should have the semantics for the segment. This process of asserting after writing a code segment is identical to the process of explaining why the segment is correct.

> If you are a student in your first programming course you will find this approach the most appealing because it allows you to separate the process of asserting code (using more formal semantics) from the process of writing the code (using your intuition). This separation is most apparent when someone else writes the code segment and then the student asserts it. Asserting after writing helps build basic knowledge and awareness of statement semantics.

Assert During

> A second approach to persuasive programming, and the next step in programming sophistication, is to assert the code as it is being written. This approach is not learned immediately.

> This process requires that you have some sense of what kind of assertions go with the various program statements. Another way of putting this is that there is a closer association between your intuitive semantic sense and the more formal description of semantics in terms of assertions.

Assert Before

> Asserting a program after it is written is useful if you are confident that the program is correct, but we would like to be able to avoid writing programs which are incorrect. The third assertion strategy is the reverse of the first.

Rather than starting with a precondition and a completed program, we start with a specification and focus on the postcondition. The strategy is to work backwards from the postcondition and figure out what statement or sequence of statements will yield the postcondition. This process is referred to as *deriving* a program from assertions and requires a good deal of intuition gained from programming experience.

Lesson 6

Semantics of Selection

This lesson focuses on the semantics of the selection statement, usually referred to by one of its standard forms, either as the "if-then" statement or the "if-then-else" statement. This type of statement is useful in programming because it makes it possible to write a more general problem solution, one which adapts to the actual data provided. An interesting observation about the selection statement is that, while the syntax is complex, the semantics is usually pretty clear to us. Perhaps it is clear because we use the selection structure so frequently in everyday conversation.

> *If I'm not there then go ahead without me.*

> *If it's sunny I'll stay; otherwise I'm heading home.*

In this lesson you will learn about the semantics of selection and appropriate ways to assert selection statements so that your code is persuasive. The lesson assumes that you have read the first four lessons of the book and that you have been introduced to the selection statement in C^{++}. A review of Boolean expressions and the material in Appendix A on logic will also be helpful.

6.1 Selection – A Brief Review

The selection statement has two forms, one an extension of the other. The two forms are illustrated in the following code segments:

```
1  if (A < B)                 1  if (A < 0)
2      distance = B - A;      2      A = (-1)*A;
3  else                       3  ...
4      distance = A - B;
5  ...
```

The first `if` statement, in which the distance between two values is determined, is commonly referred to as an "if-then-else" statement, even though in C^{++}

65

the "then" is omitted from the syntax. The Boolean expression, i.e., the if-condition, is evaluated when the statement is executed: if it evaluates to `true` the assignment statement on line 2 is executed; if the Boolean expression evaluates to `false` the assignment statement on line 4 is executed. In either case, execution continues at line 5.

The second `if` statement is similar to the first statement with the exception that there is no else-clause – this statement is commonly referred to as an "if-then" statement. For this "if-then" statement, if the Boolean expression evaluates to `true`, the statement on line 2 is executed. But if the expression evaluates to `false`, no action is taken at all. Again, in either case execution continues on line 3.

6.2   Selection Semantics – *if-then-else*

The semantics of a selection statement depends on two things: the semantic value of the Boolean expression which describes the selection condition and the semantics of the code segment(s) to be executed. This is clearly more complex than the semantics explained in previous lessons.

Consider the following if-then-else statement, which assigns a pass or fail grade based on the score received on an exam:

```
// Assert: 0 <= Score <= 100
if (Score < 60)
      Grade = 'F';
else
      Grade = 'P';
// Assert: ???
```

What is the proper way to fill in the postcondition for this statement? Just visually we can see that the only change to the state will be the value given to `Grade` – the value of `Score` doesn't change. So as a first guess we might propose the following postcondition:

```
// Assert: Grade == 'P' OR Grade == 'F'
```

This condition is certainly true – one of the two assignment statements must be executed so the value of `Grade` must be either 'P' or 'F'; i.e., the proposed postcondition must be true.

The only problem is that the postcondition does not seem to tell us enough. This rather intuitive feeling is just a reflection of the fact that the postcondition is too weak – it is satisfied by too many different states which, in fact, cannot occur. For example, the postcondition is true for the following states:

```
1.     {(Score, 70), (Grade, 'P')}
2.     {(Score, 40), (Grade, 'P')}
3.     {(Score, 70), (Grade, 'F')}
4.     {(Score, 40), (Grade, 'F')}
```

but we know that the states labelled 2 and 4 can never occur. We need a stronger condition – one which restricts the set of possible states after the selection statement.

By looking at the code we clearly see that the only way that `Grade` can have value 'P' is for `Score` to be greater than or equal to 60 – similarly we can see that `Grade` can have value 'F' only if `Score` is less than 60. This analysis leads us naturally to the following postcondition:

```
// Assert: (Score <  60  AND Grade == 'F') OR
//              (60 <= Score  AND Grade == 'P')
```

Actually, we can say a bit more if we take into account the restriction which is present in the form of the statement's precondition that the value of `Score` falls between 0 and 100. We settle on the following postcondition after factoring in the precondition:

```
// Assert: (0  <= Score < 60  AND Grade == 'F') OR
//              (60 <= Score <=100 AND Grade == 'P')
```

It is important to notice that it is not possible for the two operands of `OR` in this condition to be true simultaneously – we say the arguments are *disjoint*. This property of Boolean expressions to be disjoint will play an important role in later lessons.

Digging Deeper Into the Selection

We will take a closer look at this example and see if we can determine this postcondition, which we came by intuitively, by an alternative path. We do so by focusing on the then- and else-clauses separately and then combining our results. What will result from this investigation will be a "formula" which can be followed in determining an appropriate postcondition for a selection statement.

Looking again at our original selection statement

```
// Assert: 0 <= Score <= 100
if (Score < 60)
     Grade = 'F';
else
     Grade = 'P';
```

we notice two facts. First, the statement precondition will be true regardless of the semantic value of (`Score < 60`), so the statement precondition is true for both the then-clause and the else-clause. Second, we can push the if-condition into the precondition for the then-clause, since it must be true to reach that clause, and we can push the negation of the if-condition (`Score <= 60`) into the precondition for the else-clause for a similar reason. We have determined two conditions which must be true if the corresponding clause is reached. The following asserted code results:

```
// Assert: 0 <= Score <= 100
if (Score < 60)
    // Assert: (Score <  60) AND (0 <= Score <= 100)
    Grade = 'F';
else // Assert: (Score >= 60) AND (0 <= Score <= 100)
    Grade = 'P';
```

First, we can simplify these preconditions as follows:

```
// Assert: 0 <= Score <= 100
if (Score < 60)
    // Assert: (0 <= Score <  60)
    Grade = 'F';
else // Assert: (60 <= Score <= 100)
    Grade = 'P';
```

We can now supply postconditions based on our experience with assignment statements – notice that the clause preconditions remain true in the post-state for each assignment, so each precondition is made part of the corresponding clause postcondition:

```
// Assert: 0 <= Score <= 100
if (Score < 60)
    // Assert: (0 <= Score <  60)
    Grade = 'F';
    // Assert: (0 <= Score <  60) AND (Grade == 'F')
else // Assert: (60 <= Score <= 100)
    Grade = 'P';
    // Assert: (60 <= Score <= 100) AND (Grade == 'P')
```

And now we can see where our selection statement's postcondition comes from. We know that either the then-clause or the else-clause will be executed, and one or the other of the postconditions will be true. So joining the postconditions of the two clauses with OR, i.e., taking their disjunction, gives us the following fully asserted form:

```
// Assert: 0 <= Score <= 100
if (Score < 60)
    // Assert: (0 <= Score <  60)
    Grade = 'F';
    // Assert: (0 <= Score <  60) AND (Grade == 'F')
else // Assert: (60 <= Score <= 100)
    Grade = 'P';
    // Assert: (60 <= Score <= 100) AND (Grade == 'P')
// Assert: (0  <= Score <  60  AND Grade == 'F') OR
//         (60 <= Score <= 100 AND Grade == 'P')
```

Being More General

The pass/fail example we have just examined will lead us to two findings.
First: The example leads us to a more general statement about if-then-else semantics. Suppose that we start with the following general segment of code:

```
// Assert: S-pre
if (Condition)
     S-then;
else
     S-else;
```

where the `S-then` and `S-else` represent arbitrary segments of code (compound statements). If we follow the process used in the example above, we would arrive first at the asserted code in the left column and then, through a process of deduction, at the asserted code in the right column:

```
// Assert: S-pre           // Assert: S-pre
if (Condition)             if (Condition)
                           // Assert: S-pre AND Condition
     S-then;                   S-then;
                           // Assert: S-then-post
else                       else // Assert: S-pre AND
                           //          (NOT Condition)
     S-else;                   S-else;
                           // Assert: S-else-post
// Assert: ???             // Assert: ???
```

From this point we can deduce the selection statement's postcondition as the disjunction of the clause postconditions.

```
// Assert: S-pre
if (Condition)
     // Assert: S-pre AND Condition
     S-then;
     // Assert: S-then-post
else // Assert: S-pre AND (NOT Condition)
     S-else;
     // Assert: S-else-post
// Assert: S-then-post OR S-else-post
```

This isn't quite as straightforward as it may seem. Remember that in Lesson 5 we adopted the principle that a use of `(pre)` would always refer to the value of a variable in the pre-state of a (high-level) statement. So we must be careful in fabricating a selection postcondition in the way we have just done. We must make sure that if `S-then-post` or `S-else-post` contains a use of `(pre)` that it refers to the pre-state of the selection. Heeding this cautionary note we then have a general form for the semantics of the if-then-else statement.

Second: Our second finding, related to the first, is the realization that there is a three-step, analytical process for determining the semantics of any if-then-else statement:

1. Determine a precondition for each clause of the if-then-else statement. The precondition for the then-clause is the conjunction of the selection precondition and the selection condition; the precondition of the else-clause is the conjunction of the selection precondition and the negation of the selection condition. It is important to simplify each precondition.

   We describe this process of determining the clause preconditions as "*pushing the precondition into the selection statement.*"

   One important consequence of defining the preconditions as described is that the two preconditions are disjoint – never both true in the same state.

2. Based on each precondition, determine a postcondition for each clause. It is important that the postcondition be relative to the entire clause so that any (**pre**) in the postcondition refers to a value in the selection pre-state. By making appropriate use of (**pre**), incorporate the clause pre-condition into the postcondition.

   Again, this process will guarantee that the resulting postconditions are disjoint.

3. The selection statement's postcondition is the disjunction of the two (disjoint) clause postconditions. This construction is possible because we know that any use of (**pre**) refers to the pre-state of the selection.

Being Persuasive

Of course, the whole point of persuasive programming is to make it *easier* for a person to read and understand the programs we write. Some might claim that the asserted code above suffers from "assertion overload." We need some guidelines for how to represent selection semantics persuasively in programs.

Persuasive programming, as is true for all skills, is not developed immediately: programs you write early on will be less persuasive than programs you write later. The goal is to evolve the persuasive programming style. To help with the evolutionary process we recommend the following three levels for asserting selection statements. You should do level-1 assertions initially. When comfortable at that level move on to level-2, and then eventually to level-3.

The assertion levels are derived directly from the three analytical steps described above. As each level is described it will be illustrated using the pass/fail example above.

Level-1: Asserting at the first persuasive level is meant to focus your thoughts on the condition of the program state before each clause is executed. At this level you want to explicitly reflect in code the precondition for each clause of the if-then-else statement. This means that you carry out the first analytical step and then write the appropriate assertions. Remember the importance of simplifying expressions when possible. The pass-fail code can be asserted for this level as follows:

```
// Assert: 0 <= Score <= 100
if (Score < 60)
    // Assert: (0 <= Score <  60)
    Grade = 'F';
else // Assert: (60 <= Score <= 100)
    Grade = 'P';
```

A point to remember. There are situations where the precondition for the then-clause is identical to the statement condition (not in this case). When this is true it is acceptable to leave off the precondition for the then-clause.

Level-2: This persuasive level focuses on the condition of the program in the post-state of the clauses. At this level, then, it is appropriate to add clause postconditions to the first level asserted code. Remember that the preconditions, if defined as required, will be disjoint; so in order to guarantee that the postconditions are disjoint, you must pull the precondition through the clause statement. The following segment is a proper level-2 code segment:

```
// Assert: 0 <= Score <= 100
if (Score < 60)
    // Assert: (0 <= Score <  60)
    Grade = 'F';
    // Assert: (0 <= Score <  60) AND Grade == 'F'
else // Assert: (60 <= Score <= 100)
    Grade = 'P';
    // Assert: (60 <= Score <= 100) AND Grade == 'P'
```

Notice that there are no uses of (pre), so the warnings in the analytical process are not relevant in this example.

Level-3: This level focuses on the semantics of the selection statement as a whole, moving from the clause postconditions to a unified selection postcondition. Because we don't want to have redundant assertions, we remove the clause postconditions and put their disjunction in as the selection postcondition, illustrated as follows:

```
// Assert: 0 <= Score <= 100
if (Score < 60)
    // Assert: (0 <= Score <  60)
    Grade = 'F';
else // Assert: (60 <= Score <= 100)
    Grade = 'P';
// Assert: ( (0 <= Score <  60) AND Grade == 'F' ) OR
//         ( (60 <= Score <= 100) AND Grade == 'P' )
```

6.3   Examples

In this section we will take a detailed look at examples of selection statements in order to illustrate two things:

1. the analysis process for determining the semantics of a selection statement and

2. proper persuasive forms for each of the levels described in the previous section.

Since each persuasive level is derived from one of the steps in the semantic analysis process, we will give the proper persuasive form at the end of each analysis step.

Example 12 – Applying if-then-else semantics (I)
▼

Consider the following selection statement:

```
// Assert: X and Y have values
if (X > 10)
    Y = Y + 5;
else
    Y = Y + 10;
```

We will determine persuasive forms for each level by following the analytical process specified in the previous section.

Step 1. *Push the precondition into the selection statement – i.e., determine a precondition for each clause of the if-then-else statement. This will be the conjunction of the statement precondition and either the if-condition or the negation of the if-condition. Simplify each precondition.*

The precondition for each clause can be stated quite simply, since the precondition supplies no restrictions on the variables. Notice that since the if-condition will be the same as the then-precondition, we omit that precondition. The level-1 persuasive form follows:

```
// Assert: X and Y have values
if (X > 10)
    Y = Y + 5;
else // Assert: X <= 10
    Y = Y + 10;
```

Step 2. *Based on the set precondition, determine a postcondition for each clause. Be sure to incorporate the clause's precondition into the postcondition and simplify.*

Pulling each precondition through the corresponding assignment statement the following asserted (and persuasive) form results. Notice that the preconditions pull through intact, because the value of X does not change, consequently resulting in disjoint postconditions.

```
// Assert: X and Y have values
if (X > 10)
    Y = Y + 5;
    // Assert: (X > 10) AND Y == (pre)Y + 5
else // Assert: X <= 10
    Y = Y + 10;
    // Assert: (X <= 10) AND Y == (pre)Y + 10
```

Step 3. *The statement postcondition is the disjunction of the postconditions of the two clauses.*

```
// Assert: X and Y have values
if (X > 10)
    Y = Y + 5;
    // Assert: (X > 10) AND Y == (pre)Y + 5
else // Assert: X <= 10
    Y = Y + 10;
    // Assert: (X <= 10) AND Y == (pre)Y + 10
// Assert: ((X >  10) AND Y == (pre)Y + 5)  OR
//          ((X <= 10) AND Y == (pre)Y + 10)
```

Following the guidelines for the level-3 persuasive form, we arrive at the following final code segment:

```
// Assert: X and Y have values
if (X > 10)
    Y = Y + 5;
else // Assert: X <= 10
    Y = Y + 10;
// Assert: ((X >  10) AND Y == (pre)Y + 5)  OR
//          ((X <= 10) AND Y == (pre)Y + 10)
```

▲

Remember that the three analysis steps serve two purposes – they define a process for determining the semantics of a particular selection statement and they give a phased approach to persuasive programming. You should start out just going through the first step of the analysis. As your confidence builds, include the second and finally the third.

Example 13 – Applying if-then-else semantics (II)
▼

The following selection statement is the same as in the previous example, but now the precondition points our interest not to a postcondition involving specific values for variables, but to relative values.

```
// Assert: X >= 0 AND Y > 0
if (X > 10)
    Y = Y + 5;
else
    Y = Y + 10;
```

Step 1. *Push the precondition into the selection statement.*

The precondition for each clause can be stated and simplified as follows:

```
then:
(X >= 0 AND Y > 0) AND X > 10 ==>
    X > 10 AND Y  > 0
else:
(X >= 0 AND Y > 0) AND X <= 10 ==>
    0 <= X <= 10 AND Y  > 0
```

The following persuasive form results:

```
// Assert: X >= 0 AND Y > 0
if (X > 10)
        // Assert: X > 10 AND Y > 0
        Y = Y + 5;
else // Assert: 0 <= X <= 10 AND Y > 0
        Y = Y + 10;
```

Step 2. *Based on the set precondition, determine a postcondition for each clause. Be sure to incorporate the clause's precondition into the postcondition and simplify.*

In this example since the value of X does not change, that part of each precondition pulls through unchanged. However, the value of Y is altered, so that component of the precondition changes.

```
          // Assert: X >= 0 AND Y > 0
          if (X > 10)
              // Assert: X > 10 AND Y > 0
              Y = Y + 5;
              // Assert: X > 10 AND
              //         Y > 5 AND
              //         Y == (pre)Y+5
          else // Assert: 0 <= X <= 10 AND
              //         Y > 0
              Y = Y + 10;
              // Assert: 0 <= X <= 10 AND
              //         Y > 10 AND
              //         Y == (pre)Y+10
```

Even though part of the precondition for each clause changes in the postcondition, the two postconditions are still disjoint, since regardless of the value of Y no value of X can satisfy both.

Step 3. *The statement postcondition is the disjunction of the post-conditions of the two clauses.*

Notice the way the postcondition is formatted. The ANDs have been made to line up so that related parts of the expressions can be related. In particular, this form makes it easier to see the conditions on X which make the components of the postcondition disjoint.

```
          // Assert: X >= 0 AND Y > 0
          if (X > 10)
              // Assert: X > 10 AND Y > 0
              Y = Y + 5;
          else // Assert: 0 <= X <= 10 AND
              //         Y > 0
              Y = Y + 10;
          // Assert: (X > 10 AND
          //          Y > 5  AND
          //          Y == (pre)Y+5)
          //          OR
          //          (0 <= X <= 10 AND
          //          Y > 10 AND
          //          Y == (pre)Y+10
```

▲

Example 14 – Applying if-then-else semantics (III)
▼

Persuasively assert the following selection statement:

```
// Assert: X, Y have values

if (X < Y)
    Y = Y - X;
else
    Y = X - Y;
```

Step 1.

Since the precondition for the then-clause would be the same as the if-condition, we leave it out of the form. The precondition for the else-clause is easy, since it is just the negation of the if-condition:

```
// Assert: X, Y have values

if (X < Y)
    Y = Y - X;
else // Assert: Y <= X
    Y = X - Y;
```

Step 2.

Now things get interesting. The problem, of course, is that the value of Y changes in each clause, so just carrying the clause preconditions through to the postconditions won't work. We need to be more careful. We also must remember that we want the resulting postconditions to be disjoint.

We will first determine the postconditions the old fashioned way – we'll use (**pre**) in all appropriate places:

```
// Assert: X, Y have values

if (X < Y)
    Y = Y - X;
    // Assert: (pre)X < (pre)Y AND
    //         Y == (pre)Y - (pre)X
else // Assert: Y <= X
    Y = X - Y;
    // Assert: (pre)Y <= (pre)X AND
    //         Y == (pre)X - (pre)Y
```

From this point we can make use of the fact that X doesn't change value, so that X and (pre)X are the same. We can also add to each postcondition the fact that Y is non-negative – this follows from the fact that in each assignment statement a smaller value is being subtracted from a larger value. The following is the appropriate level-2 persuasive code:

```
// Assert: X, Y have values

if (X < Y)
     Y = Y - X;
     // Assert: X < (pre)Y AND
     //         Y == (pre)Y - X AND
     //         Y > 0
else // Assert: Y <= X
     Y = X - Y;
     // Assert: (pre)Y <= X AND
     //         Y == X - (pre)Y AND
     //         Y >= 0
```

Notice that because X < (pre)Y and (pre)Y <= X are disjoint, so are the two postconditions. But unlike previous examples, here the disjoint property requires the reference back to the pre-state.

Step 3.

Determining the final persuasive form should be straightforward from the previous step.

```
// Assert: X, Y have values

if (X < Y)
     Y = Y - X;
else // Assert: Y <= X
     Y = X - Y;
// Assert: (X < (pre)Y AND
//          Y == (pre)Y - X AND
//          Y > 0)
//          OR
//          ((pre)Y <= X AND
//           Y == X - (pre)Y AND
//           Y >= 0)
```

But there is something more here. If the fact that Y is non-negative is important, for example, if we expect to take the square root in the next statement, then we would like to make that fact more explicit. We can do this by using the distributive property of OR to "factor out" Y >= 0 from each component of the postcondition. When we do this we get a slightly weaker condition, but it does say what is important. Here is the sequence of modifications, where each one is weaker or equivalent to the previous one.

```
(X < (pre)Y AND Y == (pre)Y - X AND Y > 0)
OR
((pre)Y <= X AND Y == X - (pre)Y AND Y >= 0)

(X < (pre)Y AND Y == (pre)Y - X AND Y >= 0)
OR
((pre)Y <= X AND Y == X - (pre)Y AND Y >= 0)

(Y >= 0) AND
( (X < (pre)Y AND Y == (pre)Y - X)
  OR
  ((pre)Y <= X AND Y == X - (pre)Y) )
```

Using this, we can reassert the selection as follows, keeping in mind that the postcondition is slightly weaker than it could be.

```
// Assert: X, Y have values

if (X < Y)
     Y = Y - X;
else // Assert: Y <= X
     Y = X - Y;
// Assert: (Y >= 0) AND
//              ( (X < (pre)Y AND Y == (pre)Y - X) OR
//                ((pre)Y <= X AND Y == X - (pre)Y) )
```

In fact, if the fact that Y is non-negative is all that is important, we might leave out the second two lines of the postcondition altogether. This is, of course, completely dependent on the nature of the program where the selection statement sits.

▲

Example 15 – Applying if-then-else semantics (IV)
▼

The previous examples have avoided one important problem with the selection statement: each clause can consist of a compound statement. The purpose of this example is to illustrate that this situation is not difficult, it just takes extra care.

Persuasively assert the following selection statement:

```
// Assert: X, Y have values

if (X < Y) {
    Y = Y - X;
    X = X - Y;
}
else {
    Y = X - Y;
    X = Y - X;
}
```

Step 1.

Since the precondition for the then-clause would be the same as the if-condition, we leave it out of the form. The precondition for the else-clause is easy, since it is just the negation of the if-condition.

```
// Assert: X, Y have values

if (X < Y) {
    Y = Y - X;
    X = X - Y;
}
else { // Assert: Y <= X
    Y = X - Y;
    X = Y - X;
}
```

Step 2.

Now things get interesting. The problem, of course, is that both values X and Y change in each clause; we must take our time and pull the precondition through both assignments. We also must remember that we want the resulting postconditions to be disjoint. Happily, we will find that these concerns work through naturally.

We will first determine the postconditions by applying the technique discussed in Lesson 5.

```
// Assert: X, Y have values

if (X < Y) {
    Y = Y - X;
    X = X - Y;
}
    // Assert: (pre)X < (pre)Y        AND
    //            Y == (pre)Y - (pre)X AND
    //            X == 2*(pre)X - (pre)Y
else { // Assert: Y <= X
    Y = X - Y;
    X = Y - X;
    // Assert: (pre)Y <= (pre)X        AND
    //            Y == (pre)X - (pre)Y AND
    //            X ==   -1*(pre)Y
}
```

It is important to mention two points here:

1. The fact that the postconditions are disjoint depends on values in the selection pre-state, not the post-state.

2. By the process of Lesson 5 we know that each (pre) in the postconditions refers back to the selection pre-state – not an intermediate state in a clause.

Step 3.

Determining the final persuasive form is now straightforward. Remember that a crucial point in Lesson 5 is that the postcondition of a high-level statement should refer only to the post- and pre-states of the statement, not in a statement contained within the high-level statement.

```
// Assert: X, Y have values

if (X < Y)
    Y = Y - X;
else // Assert: Y <= X
    Y = X - Y;
// Assert: ( (pre)X < (pre)Y   AND
//             Y == (pre)Y - (pre)X AND
//             X == 2*(pre)X - (pre)Y
//           OR
//           ( (pre)Y <= (pre)X AND
//             Y == (pre)X - (pre)Y AND
//             X ==   -1*(pre)Y )
```

▲

Having invested considerable effort in understanding these relatively simple examples, we should find that the other forms of selection statement can be handled in similar ways.

6.4 Selection Semantics – *if-then*

You probably expected to see this section first in this lesson, but it turns out that the no-default case follows very easily from the with-default case. Consider the following example:

```
// Assert: (0 <= Score <= 100) AND
//          (0 <= Bonus <= 10)
if (Bonus > 5)
     Score = Score + 10;
// Assert: ???
```

We know that when (Bonus > 5) is **false** then no action is taken. But that means it is equivalent to the following selection statement:

```
// Assert: (0 <= Score <= 100) AND
//          (0 <= Bonus <= 10)
if (Bonus > 5)
     Score = Score + 10;
else
     ; // do nothing
// Assert: ???
```

Now this may look a bit weird, but what this says is that if the selection condition is false, execute the "do nothing" statement. This is a legal construction in C^{++}. Carrying out the three steps of our analysis process yields the following asserted code – we've left in all the details:

```
// Assert: (0 <= Score <= 100) AND
//          (0 <= Bonus <= 10)
if (Bonus > 5)
     // Assert:(5 <  Bonus <= 10) AND
     //          (0 <= Score <= 100)
     Score = Score + 10;
     // Assert:(5 <  Bonus <= 10)         AND
     //          (0 <= (pre)Score <= 100) AND
     //           Score == (pre)Score + 10
       // These second two lines are equivalent to
       // 10 <= Score <= 110
       // so we will use this condition instead
```

```
else
    // Assert: 0 <= Bonus <= 5 AND
    //            (0 <= Score <= 100)
    ;
    // Assert: 0 <= Bonus <= 5 AND
    //            (0 <= Score <= 100)
// Assert: ((5 <  Bonus <= 10) AND (10 <= Score <= 110)) OR
//            ((0 <= Bonus <= 5)   AND (0  <= Score <= 100))
```

We can highlight two points. First, the second argument of the OR in the postcondition is simply the negation of the if-condition along with the statement precondition; this is always the pattern for an if-then statement. Second, in the postcondition the OR has two disjoint arguments; checking the value of Bonus will indicate which range the exam score is in. Finally, we make the code more persuasive in the usual way including removing the lines associated with the unnecessary else-clause:

```
// Assert: (0 <= Score <= 100) AND
//            (0 <= Bonus <= 10)
if (Bonus > 5)
    Score = Score + 10;
// Assert: ((5 <  Bonus <= 10) AND (10 <= Score <= 110)) OR
//            ((0 <= Bonus <= 5)   AND (0  <= Score <= 100))
```

Example 16 – Update largest value
▼

Program statements do not exist in isolation. Usually there is some specific semantics in mind when a particular statement is written. Here is such a situation. There is a program in which the variable Hi is to keep track of the largest value the variable Val has had. We would like to make sure that the following code will supply the specified semantics – i.e., satisfy the postcondition Hi >= Val.

```
// Assert: Val and Hi have values
if (Val > Hi)
    Hi = Val;
```

According to the pattern just established we should assert this statement as follows:

```
// Assert: Val and Hi have values
if (Val > Hi)
    Hi = Val;
// Assert: Val > (pre)Hi AND Val == Hi) OR
//            Val <= Hi
```

What we have written is fine, as far as it goes, but there is more here. If we look at what is said about the current value of Hi (not the previous value) it is clear that we can conclude that Hi >= Val after the select statement is executed and that the previous value of Hi is either replaced by Val or is left unchanged. So we can rewrite the postcondition as follows:

```
// Assert: Val and Hi have values
if (Val > Hi)
    Hi = Val;
// Assert: Val <= Hi
```

We have verified that this if-then statement can be used to maintain the largest value of Val.

▲

Lesson 7

Semantics of Repetition

In the preface to these lessons we described a programming process termed "programming by approximation," which is characterized by a high frequency cycle of tweaking the program (often by fairly random changes) so that its execution more closely approximates the specification. Nowhere is programming by approximation more vigorously applied than in writing code for repetition statements. The initial program state, the repetition condition, the order of the statements to be repeated must all be right. There are lots of things to tweak and they are all subtly interdependent!

The purpose of this lesson is to bring a bit of order and understanding to the repetition statement. We will apply the techniques learned in the first six lessons to help analyze and understand the semantics of repetition. This lesson also assumes that you have been introduced to the while statement in C^{++}. A review of Boolean expressions and the material in Appendix A on logic will also be helpful.

7.1 Repetition – A Brief Review

The most general and best known of the repetition statements is called the while statement, or while *loop*,[1] as it is often called. While C^{++} has two other repetition statements, the for and do...while statements, we will focus in this lesson only on the while version.[2]

The following simple C^{++} while statement illustrates the common elements of all repetition statements:

---

[1]The term *loop* comes from the appearance of the graphical representation, called a *flow chart*, of the execution sequence of a repetition statement. The path of execution returns to the point of the repetition condition; this returning in the path forms a closed path or loop.

[2]The while statement is very general and, in fact, can be used to implement the other two repetition statements. The following gives the appropriate equivalences:

```
        do S while (C);    ⟹    S; while (C) { S; }
        for (I; C; A) S;   ⟹    I; while (C) { S; A; }
```

```
1  Sum = 0;
2  cin >> V;
3  while (V > 0) {
4        Sum = Sum + V;
5        cin >> V;
6  }
7  ...
```

loop initialization is responsible for initializing the program state in preparation for the repetition – in this example loop initialization involves lines 1 and 2.

loop body is the statement which is to be repeated – in this example the loop body is a compound statement which extends over lines 4 – 6.

loop condition is the Boolean expression which immediately follows the keyword `while` and determines whether to execute the next statement after the loop or to execute the loop body again – in this example the loop condition is (V > 0).

The loop in the example above sums all input values before the first non-positive input value. The loop's execution proceeds as follows. First, the initialization code is executed. Next, the loop condition is checked: if it evaluates to `false` then the loop *terminates*, and execution continues at line 7. If the loop condition evaluates to `true`, on the other hand, the statements in the loop body are executed; after line 5, execution continues at line 3: the loop condition is evaluated again, in the possibly changed state, and execution continues either at line 7 or with the loop body. This process continues until the loop condition evaluates to *false*.

7.2   Repetition Semantics

If we think of semantics in terms of the change in program state, then the semantics of repetition involves an accumulation process where the state changes from each execution of the loop body and then accumulates until the loop condition becomes false and the loop terminates. The structure of the loop and this accumulation process make the semantic description more challenging. As an example, notice that if we want to assert the loop body, it will be necessary to come up with a condition that will be true during every execution of the loop body. The purpose of this section is to come up with a strategy for determining and representing the semantics of any repetition statement.

We will start with a very simple example and determine its semantics by applying our intuitive understanding of the repetition statement:

```
// Assert: X > 0

Count   = 0;

while (Count < X) {
      Count = Count + 1;
}
// Assert: ???
```

The semantics of this statement should be indicated by finding an appropriate postcondition based on the specified precondition – i.e., we want to know what is true about the state of the program when this **while** loop terminates. In other words, we will look at everything between the two assertions as a high-level statement and determine a postcondition which refers only to the states of the program at the points of the assertions – this is in accordance with the results of Lesson 5 on the semantics of high-level statements.

Using Intuition

Intuitively, each time the loop body is executed, the value of Count is increased by 1. Since Count starts out with value 0, the value should eventually be the same as the value of X. But, when X and Count have the same value, the loop condition will evaluate to false and the loop will terminate, so we should assert the loop as follows:

```
// Assert: X > 0

Count   = 0;

while (Count < X) {
      Count = Count + 1;
}
// Assert: Count == (pre)X
```

Of course, since the value of X doesn't change in the course of execution, we can replace the (pre) simply by X.

Since one goal of persuasive programming is to focus attention on semantics, this first attempt must be seen as a success. But the other goal of persuasive programming is to facilitate explanations of code correctness. We have a postcondition for our high-level statement but have supplied no evidence of its correctness.

Digging Deeper into the Loop

In order to supply a justification of the postcondition above, we need to delve deeper into the workings of the repetition statement. We will take a more structured approach in analyzing the semantics of our counting loop.

If our goal is to provide evidence for the postcondition above, then it seems reasonable to focus on the semantics of the various parts of the loop – initialization, condition, body – and then to deduce a postcondition based on our understanding of how a loop works. We start by identifying obvious locations in the code where assertions would be useful:

```
// Assert: X > 0              loop precondition

Count = 0;

// Assert: ???                initialization postcondition
while (Count < X) {
      // Assert: ???          body precondition
      Count = Count + 1;
      //Assert: ???           body postcondition
}
// Assert: ???                loop postcondition
```

The initialization postcondition is easily supplied by appealing to the semantics of the assignment statement. It would also seem that the body precondition can be supplied easily. But we can't jump too quickly. Clearly the loop condition is always true at the beginning of the loop body since the condition must be true to enter the loop. But what about the initialization postcondition – can it be included in the body precondition? The answer is: not necessarily. It is certainly true the first time that the loop body is entered; but it is possible for the execution of the loop body to render that condition false. So adding the initialization postcondition to the body precondition is not generally done. As a starting principle, we will adopt the loop condition as the body precondition.

```
// Assert: X > 0                 loop precondition

Count = 0;

// Assert: X > 0 AND Count == 0  initialization
//                                    postcondition
while (Count < X) {
      // Assert: Count < X        body precondition
      Count = Count + 1;
      //Assert: Bpost             body postcondition
}
// Assert: Post                  loop postcondition
```

We must now determine reasonable expressions for `Bpost` and `Post`. Not surprisingly, these two conditions are closely related.

When the Loop Terminates

Generating `Bpost` is straightforward. We pull the body precondition through the assignment statement and get the following condition:

```
(pre)Count < X AND Count == (pre)Count + 1
```

By taking into account that `Count` is `(pre)Count + 1`, we can replace this condition with the following:

```
Count <= X AND Count == (pre)Count + 1
```

This leaves us with the following asserted loop:

```
// Assert: X > 0                      loop precondition

Count = 0;

// Assert: Count == 0 AND X > 0       initialization
//                                       postcondition
while (Count < X) {
        // Assert: Count < X          body precondition
        Count = Count + 1;
        //Assert: Count <= X AND      body postcondition
        //        Count == (pre)Count + 1
}
// Assert: Post                       loop postcondition
```

Now to determine `Post`. There are two factors at play here. First, we know that if we reach the postcondition, the loop condition must be false, so `Count >= X` can be one component of `Post`. The other thing we know to be true when the loop terminates is `Bpost`. We would like to include that in `Post`, but this is not possible. Remember Persuasive Principle 3 – that an occurrence of `(pre)` in a high-level statement's postcondition must refer to a value in the statement's pre-state. In `Bpost`, `(pre)Count` refers to the state at the top of the loop body, not to the value in the loop's pre-state.

We do get something from `Bpost`, however – we know at the end of the loop body that `Count <= X` is true. Since there are no occurrences of `(pre)`, we can integrate that into `Post`, yielding the following asserted form:

```
// Assert: Count == 0 AND X > 0       initialization
//                                       postcondition
while (Count < X) {
        // Assert: Count < X          body precondition
        Count = Count + 1;
        //Assert: Count <= X AND      body postcondition
        //        Count == (pre)Count + 1
}
// Assert: Count >= X AND             loop postcondition
//         Count <= X
```

The resulting postcondition is pretty useful. In fact, we can simplify it to the equivalent condition `Count == X`, which is our intuitively derived postcondition. Apparently, the other component of `Bpost` didn't add any new information. But that conclusion isn't quite fair since when we dragged the body precondition through the loop body we used the fact that `Count` is increased by 1 to obtain the condition `Count <= X`. We have arrived at the following persuasively asserted loop:

```
// Assert: X > 0                          loop precondition
Count = 0;
// Assert: Count == 0 AND X > 0           initialization
//                                            postcondition
while (Count < X) {
      // Assert: Count < X                 body precondition
      Count = Count + 1;
      //Assert: Count <= X AND             body postcondition
      //          Count == (pre)Count + 1
}
// Assert: Count == X                      loop postcondition
```

An Alternate Approach – Unwinding

While our work in the previous section ended with the result we wanted – i.e., a persuasively asserted statement – you may feel a bit uneasy about just dropping that final bit of the body's postcondition. Was it really okay to just ignore it?

We need to dig a bit deeper into the workings of the loop, and the best way to do this is to "unwind" the loop. This means to choose a particular value for X — say 3 – and then replace the loop by that many repetitions of the code in the loop body. Here is an unwinding for our example. Notice how the body pre- and postconditions are wrapped around the body code at each step:

```
// Assert: X == 3
Count = 0;

// Assert: Count < X
Count = Count + 1;
// Assert: Count == (per)Count + 1 == (0) + 1

// Assert: Count < X
Count = Count + 1;
// Assert: Count == (per)Count + 1 == (0 + 1) + 1

// Assert: Count < X
Count = Count + 1;
// Assert: Count == (per)Count + 1 == (0 + 1 + 1) + 1

// Assert: Count == X
```

There are two things we can learn from this unwinding process. First, we see that the loop initialization affects only the first pass through the loop body. Okay, this isn't surprising, but it does show why we can't move the initialization's postcondition into the loop body's precondition!

The second thing we learn from the unwinding is how the value of `Count` accumulates with each execution of the loop body. When the loop body's post-condition reads as follows,

```
Count = Count + 1;
//Assert: Count <= X AND
//        Count == (pre)Count + 1
```

the accumulation is actually represented, but in a somewhat hidden way – `(pre)Count` represents the value of `Count` at the previous assertion, which was either its initial value of 0 or the result from the previous pass – so `(pre)Count` is an implicit representation of the part of `Count` accumulated over the *previous* executions of the loop body. By unwinding we see this fact explicitly. This is an easy and often illuminating technique to use.

But what good does this unwinding ultimately do? We can rewrite the condition reflecting `Count`'s value making use of the unwinding,

```
Count == 1 + ... + 1
```

where the number of 1s is equal to the number of passes made through the loop body. This "number of passes made through the loop" is an important value – it would be convenient to have access to it. Since our work is purely descriptive (i.e., not part of the program) we will adopt a new bit of notation to use in assertions,

```
(R)
```

which will denote a counter whose value is the "number" of the current loop body execution – as though `(R)` were a hidden variable and each loop had the following structure:

```
(R) = 0;
while (...) {
      (R) = (R) + 1;
      ....
}
```

With this in mind, notice that in the previous counting loop example, the value of `Count` (after it is incremented) is always the same as `(R)`. We will find that sometimes `(R)` is essential to expressing a loop's semantics – other times it will be of no use at all. Making use of this new notation we can rewrite our body postcondition as follows:

```
Count = Count + 1;
//Assert: Count <= X AND
//        Count == 1+...+1   (R) times
```

Notice that the use of (R) makes the accumulation of body executions explicit.

We now have a body postcondition which references only the current program state. This means that the body post can be directly incorporated into Post.

```
// Assert: Count >= X AND
//         Count <= X AND
//         Count == (R)
```

And when we simplify the first two components to get Count == X, we see that all three values — Count, X, and (R) — are the same.

What should we make of this new notation (R)? First, since it is a hidden variable associated with the loop, it is apparently irrelevant as we move to the program code after the loop. This should indicate that it is probably a good idea to keep it out of the loop postcondition. On the other hand, it appears to be a very good tool for analyzing what happens in a loop – especially if we unwrap a loop. The notation (R) allows us to represent explicitly what has gone on in the previous passes through the loop body.

Being More General

Based on our experience with the previous example, we should be able to come up with a basic strategy for analyzing the semantics of a repetition statement. Consider the following general form for a while loop:

```
// Assert: loop precondition
I; // loop initialization

while (condition)
        S; // loop body

// Assert: ???
```

Our very general strategy remains the same as in Lesson 5: we take the loop precondition and pull it through the loop initialization and the resulting condition through the loop. What we will have in the end is the loop postcondition.

The first step in analyzing the loop is to determine a postcondition for the initialization and a precondition for the loop body. The loop body precondition can be taken to be simply the loop condition. We determine the initialization postcondition by pulling the loop precondition through the high-level statement I.

In the second step we determine the postcondition for the loop body. This can be done either by applying existing semantic analysis or by unwinding the loop to determine how values accumulate as a result of executing the loop. It is essential in this to find a body postcondition which is free of (pre) references – the use of the hidden variable (R) is useful in this regard. Notice that this step is midway in the process of pulling the initialization postcondition through the loop.

These two steps can be summarized in the following display, where the left column represents the result of the first step and the right column the result of adding the second step:

```
// Assert: loop precondition    // Assert: loop precondition
I;                              I;
// Assert: init post            // Assert: init post
while (condition)               while (condition)
        // Assert: condition            // Assert: condition
        S;                              S;
                                        // Assert: body
                                        //         postcondition

// Assert: ???                  // Assert: ???
```

Finally, we complete the task of pulling the initialization postcondition through the loop. Having determined a body postcondition which is free from (pre) references, we can determine the loop's postcondition. In the counting example above, determining the loop postcondition was easy – it was just the conjunction of the body postcondition and the negation of the loop condition. But in that example we knew that the loop body always executed at least once (since X was known to be positive). But this is not always the case. If the loop condition is false on the first evaluation, then the loop body never executes. In this case loop post remains true and the loop condition is false. Since there are two possible situations – the loop body is or is not executed – the postcondition must be the disjunction of the two conditions. Putting it in terms of "pulling," when pulling a condition through a loop there are two alternate paths: one which passes through the loop body at least once and one which does not. The postcondition must reflect pulling along each of these paths. The final asserted code is the result:

```
// Assert: loop precondition
I; // loop initialization
// Assert: init post
while (condition)
        // Assert: condition
        S; // loop body
        // Assert: body postcondition
// Assert: (NOT condition) AND
//         ( (init post) OR
//           (body postcondition)
//         )
```

This not only gives us a general form for the semantics of a repetition statement, it also gives us a three-step, analytical process for determing the semantics of any specific repetition statement.

1. Pull the loop precondition through the loop initialization to determine the initialization postcondition.

2. Use the loop condition as the precondition for the loop body and pull this condition through the loop body to determine the body postcondition. Use unwinding and the hidden variable (R) to determine a postcondition free of (pre) references.

3. Determine a postcondition for the loop by taking the conjunction of the negation of the loop condition and the disjunction of the initialization postcondition and the body's postcondition. Simplify this postcondition.

Being Persuasive

The analytical process described above will have a tendency to generate a lot of assertions – the abundance of assertions may even obscure the reasoning present in the assertions. But the analysis is essential for determining the semantics. Having done the analysis, we need a strategy to turn the result of the analytical steps into persuasive code.

It is also important to realize that learning to write persuasive programs takes time and experience. It is important for you to have assertion strategies to fit your current understanding of repetition semantics. To help with the learning process, we recommend the following three levels for asserting repetition statements. You should concentrate on level-1 assertions initially and then move on to level-2 and level-3 as your semantic understanding and confidence increase.

The assertion levels are influenced by the three analytical steps described in the previous section. As each level is described it will be illustrated using the counting example discussed above.

Level-1: The first level is meant to focus attention on the most basic aspects of semantics: a postcondition for the initialization, a precondition for the loop body (the same as the loop condition) and the simplest form for the loop postcondition, i.e., the negation of the loop condition:

```
// Assert: X > 0

Count = 0;

// Assert: Count == 0 AND X > 0
while (Count < X) {
        // Assert: Count < X
        Count = Count + 1;
}
// Assert: Count >= X
```

Level-2: The second level focuses on the semantics of the loop body. This means that the level-1 asserted code is augmented by a postcondition for the loop body. This postcondition can be arrived at by conventional means or by unwinding. At this level it is acceptable to drop the loop precondition, since it is just a copy of the loop condition:

```
// Assert: X > 0

Count = 0;

// Assert: Count == 0 AND X > 0
while (Count < X) {
        Count = Count + 1;
        // Assert: Count <= X AND
        //             Count == 1+...+1 (R) times
}
// Assert: Count >= X
```

Level-3: At this level we add to the simplified form of the postcondition as described in the analysis above:

```
// Assert: X > 0

Count = 0;

// Assert: Count == 0 AND X > 0
while (Count < X) {
        Count = Count + 1;
        // Assert: Count <= X AND
        //             Count == 1+...+1 (R) times
}
// Assert: Count == X
```

7.3 Asserting a Loop – A First Example

Here is a **while** loop which sums the first X positive integers – when X is 5, the final value of Sum should be $0 + 1 + 2 + 3 + 4 + 5 = 15$:

```
// Assert: X > 0

Count = 0;
Sum   = 0;

while (Count < X) {
        Count = Count + 1;
        Sum = Sum + Count;
}
// Assert: ???
```

Let's try our method on this loop to see what we discover. We will go through the example using the three-step analysis and at each step will indicate the appropriate persuasive code.

Step 1. *Determine the postcondition for the loop initialization.*

The loop initialization simply sets initial values for the variables Sum and Count. Pulling the initialization precondition through these two assignments yields the following postcondition:

```
// Assert: X > 0

Count = 0;
Sum   = 0;


// Assert: Count == 0 AND Sum == 0 AND X > 0
```

This first analytical step is straightforward. To get the appropriate level-1 persuasive code we add a precondition for the loop body and determine the simplest of loop postconditions.

```
// Assert: X > 0

Count = 0;
Sum   = 0;
// Assert: X > 0 AND Count == 0 AND Sum == 0
while (Count < X) {
        //Assert: Count < X
        Count = Count + 1;
        Sum   = Sum + Count;
}
// Assert: Count >= X
```

Step 2. *Using the loop condition as the precondition for the loop body, determine a postcondition for the loop body and simplify.*

We want to complete the postcondition for this segment of code:

```
//Assert: Count < X
Count = Count + 1;
Sum   = Sum + Count;
// Assert: ???
```

Traditional Approach

If we take the traditional approach and apply compound and assignment statement semantics, then we can immediately write the complete postcondition as follows:

```
//Assert: Count < X
Count = Count + 1;
Sum   = Sum + Count;
// Assert: (pre)Count < X AND
//         Count == (pre)Count + 1 AND
//         Sum   == (pre)Sum + Count
```

The one bit of simplification we can carry out here is the comparison of (pre)Count and X. Since Count is less than X in the pre-state and Count is incremented by one, we can deduce that Count is less than *or equal to* X in the post-state. In this way we get the following persuasive code:

```
// Assert: X > 0

Count = 0;
Sum   = 0;
// Assert: X > 0 AND Count == 0 AND Sum == 0
while (Count < X) {
      Count = Count + 1;
      Sum   = Sum + Count;
      // Assert: Count <= X AND
      //         Count == (pre)Count + 1 AND
      //         Sum   == (pre)Sum + Count
}
// Assert: Count >= X
```

While this is a fine postcondition, remember that it has one drawback: because (pre) appears in the postcondition, it cannot be used in the loop's postcondition (Persuasive Principle 3).

Unwinding Approach

But we can also try the method of unwinding, which will hopefully lead us to a (pre)-free postcondition. If we assume that the value of X is 3, then we get the following unwinding:

```
// Assert: X == 3

Count = 0;
Sum   = 0;

Count = Count + 1;
Sum = Sum + Count;
      //Assert: Count <= X AND
      //        Count == 0 + 1 AND
      //        Sum   == 0 + 1

// Assert: Count < X
Count = Count + 1;
Sum = Sum + Count;
      //Assert: Count <= X AND
      //        Count == 0 + 1 + 1 AND
      //        Sum   == 0 + 1 + 2
```

```
// Assert: Count < X
Count = Count + 1;
Sum = Sum + Count;
    //Assert: Count <= X AND
    //         Count == 0 + 1 + 1 + 1 AND
    //         Sum   == 0 + 1 + 2 + 3

// Assert: Count == X
```

By making use of the adopted hidden variable (R) we can simplify this to the following:

```
// Assert: X == 3

Count = 0;
Sum   = 0;

Count = Count + 1;
Sum = Sum + Count;
    //Assert: Count <= X AND
    //         Count == (R) AND
    //         Sum   == 0 +...+ Count

// Assert: Count < X
Count = Count + 1;
Sum = Sum + Count;
    //Assert: Count <= X AND
    //         Count == (R) AND
    //         Sum   == 0 +...+ Count

// Assert: Count < X
Count = Count + 1;
Sum = Sum + Count;
    //Assert: Count <= X AND
    //         Count == (R) AND
    //         Sum   == 0 +...+ Count

// Assert: Count == X
```

By rewriting this unwinding in terms of (R), we can clearly see the appropriate pattern for the postcondition:

```
// Assert: X > 0

Count = 0;
Sum   = 0;
// Assert: X > 0 AND Count == 0 AND Sum == 0
while (Count < X) {
        Count = Count + 1;
        Sum   = Sum + Count;
        // Assert: Count <= X AND
        //         Count == (R) AND
        //         Sum == 1 +...+ Count
}
// Assert: Count >= X
```

We now have a body postcondition which is free from references to (**pre**), so it should be useful in the final step.

Step 3. *Determine a postcondition for the loop by taking the conjunction of the negation of the loop condition and the body's postcondition. Simplify this postcondition.*

Making use of the body postcondition found in step 2, we can write the following for the loop postcondition:

```
// Assert: Count >= X AND
//         Count <= X AND
//         Count == (R) AND
//         Sum   == 1 +...+ Count
```

But we can simplify this condition quite a bit. The first two lines are equivalent to Count == X. Because of this equality we can replace Count with X in the final line. As in the previous example we can ignore the third line because we have already deduced a more useful value for Count in terms of X. These simplifications give us the following as loop postcondition:

```
// Assert: Count == X AND
//         Sum   == 1 +...+ X
```

One final comment on this postcondition. It is common with loops to use certain variables within the loop in a purely temporary way – the variable Count in the example illustrates this use. If a variable is used purely to aid in the loop computation and is not used in program statements following the loop, then the variable need not appear in the loop postcondition. Remember, since a statement postcondition will be the precondition for the next statement, if the variable is relevant only to the first statement, its condition is not relevant to the next statement. For this reason it is reasonable to drop the variable Count in the following persuasive version of the code:

```
// Assert: X > 0

Count = 0;
Sum   = 0;
// Assert: X > 0 AND Count == 0 AND Sum == 0
while (Count < X) {
        Count = Count + 1;
        Sum   = Sum + Count;
        // Assert: Count <= X AND
        //              Sum   == 1 +...+ Count
}
// Assert: Sum == 1 +...+ X
```

7.4   Asserting a Loop – Input Examples

A common use of repetition is in data input. In this section we will look at the following problem. We are interested in writing a code segment which can be used to provide guaranteed valid keyboard input from a user. In particular, an upper bound and a lower bound are supplied and values are repeatedly input until a value entered falls between the two bounds. A careful examination of the following pre- and postconditions should convince you that they accurately describe what is required:

```
// Pre:  Low <= Hi
//            AND
//        input stream == <v0,...,vn,r,...>
//            AND
//        ((v0 < Low OR v0 > Hi) AND
//            ...                   AND
//         (v(n-1) < Low OR v(n-1) > Hi))
//            AND
//        (Low <= vn <= Hi)

// Post: V == vn                   AND
//        input stream == <r,...>       AND
//        (pre)Low <= V <= (pre)Hi
```

Just to review these conditions line by line:

line 1: Low and Hi define an input interval.

line 2: The input stream initially has n values, namely v1 through vn.

line 3: The first (n) of the input values fall outside of the interval specified by Low and Hi.

line 4: The (n+1) value on the input stream, vn, does fall within the specified interval.

The postcondition is simpler to read, especially understanding what the precondition says. The postcondition basically says that the first (n-1) input values are discarded and the nth one is saved in the variable V and that V falls between the originally specified interval boundaries.

It is claimed that the following code segment will have the semantics specified by the pre- and postconditions above:

```
// Assert:  Low <= Hi
//              AND
//          input stream == <v0,...,vn,r,...>
//              AND
//          ((v0 < Low OR v0 > Hi) AND
//              ...                    AND
//           (v(n-1) < Low OR v(n-1) > Hi))
//              AND
//          (Low <= vn <= Hi)

cout << "Enter >> ";
cin  >> V;
while ( (V < Low) || (V > Hi) ) {
      cout << "Enter >> ";
      cin  >> V;
}
```

Our job is to appropriately assert this code to see whether the claim for the code is valid. Before proceeding with the analysis of this code segment, notice that the values of Low and Hi are not changed in the code. Also, the conditions in the third and fourth lines of the assertion remain true throughout the execution of the code. In order to hold down assertion clutter, we will leave these components out of subsequent assertions but remember that they are true.

Step 1. *Determine the postcondition for the loop initialization.*

Dragging the initial assertion through the initialization code, we find that the first value, v1, is removed from the input stream and assigned to V.

```
// Assert: Low <= Hi
//              AND
//          input stream == <v1,...,vn,r,...>
//              AND
//          ((v0 < Low OR v0 > Hi) AND
//              ...                    AND
//           (v(n-1) < Low OR v(n-1) > Hi))
//              AND
//          (Low <= vn <= Hi)

cout << "Enter >> ";
cin  >> V;
// Assert: V == v0
```

We should be mindful that the first value, v0, may in fact be the valid one –
i.e., that n == 0. In this case the loop body will not be executed, but we will
revisit this situation in the third step.

Step 2. *Determine a postcondition for the loop body.*

We proceed as in the previous example by unwinding the loop to see what
pattern of behavior emerges. In this case, however, we will unwind the loop
only partially. In other words, we won't fix a size of the input stream but will
just unwind the first three passes through the loop body:

```
cout << "Enter >> ";
cin  >> V;
// Assert: V == v0 AND input stream == <v1,...,vn,r,...>

// Assert: V < Low OR V > Hi
cout << "Enter >> ";
cin  >> V;
// Assert: V == v1 AND input stream == <v2,...,vn,r,...>

// Assert: V < Low OR V > Hi
cout << "Enter >> ";
cin  >> V;
// Assert: V == v2 AND input stream == <v3,...,vn,r,...>

// Assert: V < Low OR V > Hi
cout << "Enter >> ";
cin  >> V;
// Assert: ???
```

What is common across each of these steps? If we remember that the hidden
variable (R) is just the step number, then we can see the body postcondition
emerging – after each input we can state the following:

```
// Assert: V < Low OR V > Hi
cout << "Enter >> ";
cin  >> V;
// Assert: V == v(R) AND input stream == <v((R)+1),...,n>
```

That notation "V(R)" and "V((R)+1)" looks looks a bit odd, but its meaning
should be clear. We can gain more clarity if we focus on the final incomplete
assertion. At that point we know that the V == v(R) (and that (R) is 3), but
we are unsure whether this new value of V is valid or not – we won't know until
the loop condition is checked. So at that point (the bottom of the loop body)
we can say that (R) <= n. This seems to carry all the information that the
condition

```
input stream == <v((R)+1),...,n>
```

carries, but with greater clarity. Here is the resulting asserted loop body:

```
// Assert: V < Low OR V > Hi
cout << "Enter >> ";
cin  >> V;
// Assert: V == v(R) AND (R) <= n
```

Making use of these findings, then, we can provide the following level-2 persuasive code:

```
// Assert: Low <= Hi
//              AND
//          input stream == <v1,...,vn,r,...>
//              AND
//          ((v0 < Low OR v0 > Hi) AND
//                  ...              AND
//           (v(n-1) < Low OR v(n-1) > Hi))
//              AND
//          (Low <= vn <= Hi)

cout << "Enter >> ";
cin  >> V;
// Assert: V == v0
while ( (V < Low) || (V > Hi) ) {
      cout << "Enter >> ";
      cin  >> V;
      // Assert: V == v(R) AND (R) <= n
}
```

Step 3. *Determine a postcondition for the loop.*

In the previous step we determined a body postcondition which is free of references to (pre). This means that the loop postcondition should be easy to structure. We recall that when the loop executes there are two paths to consider – one in which the loop body is not executed and the other in which the loop body is executed at least one time. The result is the following loop postcondition:

```
// Assert: Low <= V <= Hi               AND
//          ( (V == v0 AND n == 0) OR
//            (V == v(R) AND (R) <= n) )
```

We can simplify this in a couple of ways. First, the only way that (R) < n can be true is for the value v(R) to be invalid. But this would mean that V would not fall within the interval specified by Low and Hi. So it must be that (R) == n is true. If we rewrite the postcondition based on this conclusion we will see that more simplification is possible:

```
// Assert: Low <= V <= Hi               AND
//          ( (V == v0 AND n == 0) OR
//            (V == vn) )
```

Now we see that with n == 0, we can rewrite the condition again:

```
// Assert: Low <= V <= Hi AND
//           V == vn
```

One final adjustment is possible. As the program continues execution beyond the loop, the fact that the value of V falls in the specified range is what is important – the fact that V has the specific value vn is not important. What is important, and reflects a connection to vn, however, is the fact that at the end of the loop the input stream has had all the values v0 through vn removed. We can now give the final persuasively asserted form for the input loop:

```
// Assert: Low <= Hi
//           AND
//           input stream == <v1,...,vn,r,...>
//           AND
//           ((v0 < Low OR v0 > Hi) AND
//             ...                      AND
//            (v(n-1) < Low OR v(n-1) > Hi))
//           AND
//           (Low <= vn <= Hi)

cout << "Enter >> ";
cin  >> V;
// Assert: V == v0
while ( (V < Low) || (V > Hi) ) {
      cout << "Enter >> ";
      cin  >> V;
      // Assert: V == v(R) AND (R) <= n
}
// Assert: Low <= V <= Hi AND
//           input stream == <r,...>
```

The Code Is Verified

So have we met the specification given by the pre- and postconditions at the beginning of this section? If we examine the original postcondition,

```
// Post: V == vn
//         input stream == <r,...>
//         (pre)Low <= V <= (pre)Hi
```

we can easily see that it is satisfied. There's an interesting connection here between persuasive programming and verifying a code fragment. In producing the persuasive version of the code, we eliminated the reference in the postcondition to vn because it would not be relevant to the code which follows the loop. But when we talk about verifying a code fragment, we are focused on the fragment alone – the fact that vn is the last value of V is important to that verification.

Lesson 8

Semantics of Abstraction

Abstraction in a programming language is the use of an identifier in place of a segment of code (the identifier *abstracts* the code).[1] There are two basic abstraction mechanisms: a *procedure* is the abstraction of a sequence of statements (in C^{++} this is a function with void return type), while a *function* is the abstraction of an expression (i.e., it computes a value). Abstraction can be thought of as a mechanism for adding new commands to a language – new commands that the programmer defines. Our interest in this lesson is the semantics of abstraction and how it can be represented in terms of assertions. We start with a brief review of the syntactic structures associated with abstraction and then turn to the semantics of defining and applying abstraction. Also, in this lesson we will focus on procedural abstraction, saving comments on functional abstraction for the last section of the lesson.

For this lesson we expect that you have been introduced to function definition in C^{++} for both procedural and functional abstractions and the use of parameters, both value and reference. We also expect that you have been introduced to function calls and the difference between actual and formal parameters.

8.1 Abstraction – A Brief Review

This section provides a review of the basic ideas behind the use of abstraction. If you are very familiar with these ideas it is still a good idea to skim over the section to see what terminology is used dealing with abstraction in this and the remaining lessons.

There are two aspects to an abstraction. First, each abstraction must be defined – this means associating an identifier with a list of parameters (the formal parameters) and a segment of code. In C^{++} there is also a requirement to specify a return type; void is used for procedural abstractions, and a

---

[1] Actually there are two basic forms of abstraction: code abstraction and data abstraction. In these lessons we will always use *abstraction* to refer to code abstraction and *data abstraction* in the other case.

data type (other than void) is used for functional abstraction. The following code segment illustrates a procedural abstraction, QuotRem, and a functional abstraction, GetData:

```
void QuotRem (int Num, int Div, int & Quot, int & Rem) {

      Quot = Num / Div;
      Rem  = Num % Div;
}

int GetData() {

      int v;
      cout << "Enter an integer value >> ";
      cin  >> v;
      return v;
}
```

The identifier QuotRem is associated with four formal parameters and a segment of code consisting of two assignment statements. The list of formal parameters illustrates the two kinds of parameters – those with & in front of the identifier are reference parameters (Quot and Rem) and the other two (Num and Div) are called value parameters. The identifier GetData is associated with no parameters, a segment of four statements and the return type int. Notice that the special statement **return** indicates that the value to be returned by the abstraction is the value of the local variable v, which has the same type as the abstraction's specified return type.

The second aspect of abstraction is referencing an abstraction, commonly referred to as *calling* an abstraction. The following code segment contains three examples of abstraction calls:

```
1   void main() {

2        int X, Y, Q, R;
3        X = GetData();
4        Y = GetData();
5        QuotRem (X, Y, Q, R);
         . . .
    }
```

Line 5 illustrates a call to a procedural abstraction. It takes the form of an imperative statement – the abstraction's name is used and followed by a list of actual parameters to be associated with the formal parameters in the definition. Lines 3 and 4 illustrate calls to a functional abstraction. Again the name is used and followed by a list of actual parameters. In this case, since the definition of GetData specifies no formal parameters, no actual parameters are specified. The interesting thing about a call to a functional abstraction is that it appears not as a separate statement, but as an element in an expression.

It is also important to recognize the significance of the value and reference parameters of QuotRem. The fact that X and Y correspond to the value parameters Num and Div, respectively, means that the values of X and Y will remain unchanged when the abstraction QuotRem returns. The other two parameters, Q and R, on the other hand, correspond to the reference parameters Quot and Rem. When the call to QuotRem returns, the values of Q and R will be the same as the final values of Quot and Rem before the return.

Another thing that happens when calling an abstraction is the establishment of a separate environment – the environment defined by the declarations (including the formal parameters) within the code segment of the abstraction. From the example above, the main program has an environment with four variables – X, Y, Q, and R. The abstraction QuotRem defines its own environment, which includes four formal parameters: Num, Div, Quot, and Rem. When the abstraction is called, the abstraction's environment temporarily replaces (shadows) that of the calling environment. When GetData is called, the new environment includes just one *local* variable v – there are no parameters.

8.2 Semantics of Abstraction

Suppose that you want an abstraction named GetSolution that will find the solution to any equation of the form $ax + b = 0$, where a and b are integer values. Exactly how this abstraction is to be implemented may not be exactly clear at this point, but it is pretty clear what the effect of calling this abstraction will be — the following code segment, complete with pre- and postconditions, illustrates a call:

```
int   A, B; // coefficients in the equation
float Solution;
...
// Assert:  A != 0 AND B has a value
GetSolution(A, B, Solution);
// Assert:  A*Solution + B == 0
...
```

These pre- and postconditions illustrate what we mean by the *intended semantics* of an abstraction. Notice that, knowing division by zero leads to an error, we have restricted the value of A that can be passed to the abstraction — we have put no such restriction on the value of B. The assertion after the call indicates the relationship that must exist among the three variables after the return.

It is the programmer's job to guarantee that when the abstraction is implemented (i.e., when a formal parameter list and code segment have been specified), the *inherent semantics* of the code segment for the abstraction matches the intended semantics. You have probably noticed that these notions of intended and inherent semantics are similar to the user's and programmer's views of a program, which we discussed in Lesson 2.

The Intended Semantics of an Abstraction

Consider the partial definition in the following code segment of the abstraction `GetSolution`, which we have just discussed:

```
void GetSolution (int A, int B, float & S) {

    // code to be filled in
}
```

The first line of the definition gives a general description of how to call this abstraction – use the name `GetSolution` and three actual parameters, the first two being value parameters and the third a reference parameter. Of course, what we don't know from this incomplete code is how these parameters will be used. But that is exactly the point of the intended semantics – to state what the user expects to happen when the abstraction is called. If we associate pre- and postconditions with this first line, then we have something we can use to advertise the (intended) functionality of the abstraction `GetSolution`. Here is a new description of the abstraction complete with pre- and postconditions written using the environment defined by the formal parameter list:

```
void GetSolution (int A, int B, float & S)
        // Pre:  A != 0 AND B has a value
        // Post: A*S + B == 0
```

Another way to think of the intended semantics of an abstraction is as a contract with the person(s) who will use (i.e., call) the abstraction. This contract implies that the intended semantics will match the actual semantics.

When we look at the original code containing the call to `GetSolution` we see that things fit pretty well together:

```
int   A, B;
float Solution;
...
// Assert:  A != 0 AND B has a value
GetSolution(A, B, Solution);
// Assert:  A*Solution + B == 0
...
```

The pre- and postconditions are derived from the interface by substituting each actual parameter for its corresponding formal parameter. Notice that the interface specifies the first two parameters as value parameters, so the corresponding actual parameters will not change. At the same time, since the third parameter is a reference parameter, the postcondition implies a new restriction on the value of `S` after the call.

There is one possible source of confusion when specifying the intended semantics of an abstraction. We know that the identifiers in the precondition stand for values when the abstraction is called – they are initial values. But in the postcondition the `A`, `B`, and `S` refer to final values. We will adopt the following convention: in the postcondition, when referring to the *final* value of a reference parameter, we will prefix (out) to the identifier. When referring to the *initial* value of any parameter, we will prefix (in) to the identifier. Following this convention, we restate the intended semantics of GetSolution as follows:

```
void GetSolution (int A, int B, float & S) {
    // Pre:   A != 0 AND B has a value
    // Post:  (in)A*(out)S + (in)B == 0
```

Remember the importance of the precondition for GetSolution. If this precondition is not met, then the whole purpose of the abstraction is defeated. In fact, we should assume that if the precondition is not met, the abstraction will not function as advertised. Think of what happens if you make a call to sqrt and pass it a negative parameter. (If you haven't tried this, take a minute and do so.) Either the program will crash, due to some computational error, or some nonsensical value will be produced. In either case the result is not the square root of the parameter. It is up to the programmer to guarantee that the abstraction's precondition is met at the point of each call to the abstraction so that the potential failure can be avoided.

Example 17 – Finding the quotient and remainder
▼

At the beginning of this lesson the following abstraction definition occurs:

```
void QuotRem (int Num, int Div, int & Quot, int & Rem) {

    Quot = Num / Div;
    Rem  = Num % Div;
}
```

This abstraction returns, via the reference parameters Quot and Rem, the quotient and remainder when the parameter Num is divided by Div. Easy enough to say, but how should it be described in terms of pre- and postconditions? How should we define the interface for QuotRem to accurately describe the intended semantics?

To come up with an interface we need to focus on the value parameters for the precondition and the reference parameters for the postcondition. For the value parameters there should be no restriction on the value of Num, but since division by zero is not allowed we should restrict the value of Div. It will also be convenient to require that both value parameters be non-negative. The following precondition specifies these conditions:

```
// Pre:   Num >= 0 AND Div > 0
```

How about the postcondition for this abstraction? We could try to write down a specific value for each reference parameter, but in this case and many others it is easier to describe both of the values in terms of a single relationship, namely that the value of Num is the same as Quot times Div plus Rem. Here is a possible postcondition for QuotRem, making use of the (in)/(out) notation described above:

```
// Post: (in)Num = (out)Quot*(in)Div + (out)Rem
```

But we've missed the mark here – just slightly. There are too many solutions that can satisfy this postcondition.

```
{Num = 15, Div = 4, Quot = 2, Rem = 7}
```

```
{Num = 15, Div = 4, Quot = 3, Rem = 3}
```

The first of these is clearly not one we would expect; the second is. We must make the postcondition stronger. Since the problem seems to be with the value of Rem, we should restrict the values it can take. In fact, we want the value of Rem to be as small as possible; that is, we must require Rem to be less than Div. Here, then, is the interface we want, complete with the improved (stronger) postcondition:

```
void QuotRem (int Num, int Div, int & Quot, int & Rem)

    // Pre:   Num >= 0 AND Div > 0
    // Post: (in)Num = (out)Quot*(in)Div + (out)Rem
    //           AND
    //         0 <= (out)Rem < (in)Div
```

▲

   The pre- and postconditions for an abstraction define what values are acceptable as value parameters and what values (if any) will be returned by the abstraction via the reference parameters. The first step in writing any abstraction should be writing the pre- and postconditions. These should give a precise description of the abstraction's intended semantics.

The Inherent Semantics of an Abstraction

The notion of inherent semantics of an abstraction is exactly analogous to that of inherent semantics of a program. Inherent semantics refers to the semantics of the statements that are there rather than the semantics we want. When a programmer implements an abstraction, i.e., supplies a code segment, it is important for the programmer to believe that the code supplied actually meets the interface as described by the abstraction's pre- and postconditions. So after implementing an abstraction, the programmer should verify that the inherent semantics of the abstraction's code segment is the same as the intended semantics of the abstraction. We can see how this might work by returning to Example 17 above.

Here is the definition for `QuotRem` as given without the pre- and postconditions:

```
void QuotRem (int Num, int Div, int & Quot, int & Rem) {

    Quot = Num / Div;
    Rem  = Num % Div;
}
```

The idea is to show that the semantics of the two assignment statements, assuming the precondition, is the same as the postcondition we determined before. We look at this one statement at a time.

```
Quot = Num / Div;
```

We know that the right side of this assignment statement is an expression involving integer division – this means that when `Div` is divided into `Num` we get as result the result of dividing with the remainder discarded – we also know that that remainder thrown away is non-zero but less than `Div`. We can assert the first assignment statement as follows:

```
// Assert: Num >= 0 AND Div > 0
Quot = Num / Div;
// Assert: Num >= 0 AND Div > 0 AND Quot == Num/Div
//         -- Num/Div denotes integer division
```

The first two components of the postcondition come through because we know the values of `Num` and `Div` have not changed. The last line of the postcondition is just a reminder about the use of integer division.

```
Rem = Num % Div;
```

The semantics here depend on the meaning of the `%` operator, better known as the mod operator. The mod operator is well-known and very useful in computing; it gives the remainder that results when dividing the first argument by the second. So we can assert this statement as follows:

```
// Assert: Num >= 0 AND Div > 0  AND Quot == Num/Div
//         -- Num/Div denotes integer division
Rem = Num % Div;
// Assert: Rem == Num - (Num/Div)*Div AND
//         0 <= Rem < Div
//         -- Num/Div denotes integer division
```

But the postcondition we have here is derived directly from the definition of mod. If we take advantage of what is stated in the precondition, namely

```
       Quot == Num/Div
```

and the fact that `Quot` does not change as a result of the execution, we can rewrite the postcondition as

```
       // Assert: Rem == Num - Quot*Div AND
       //               0 <= Rem < Div
```

By simplifying the first line of this postcondition and following the advice on asserting sequences of statements (Section 5) we arrive at the following semantics for the two assignment statements:

```
       // Assert: Num >= 0 AND Div > 0
       Quot = Num / Div;
       Rem = Num % Div;
       // Assert: Num == Quot*Div + Rem AND
       //               0 <= Rem < Div
```

Looking back at the interface specified for the abstraction `QuotRem`, we see that the pre- and postconditions just determined match exactly.

We have determined the inherent semantics for the abstraction code segment and found that they match the intended semantics of the abstraction – we conclude that the implementation of the abstraction is a correct one. In a sense, we have verified that the contract with the user of this abstraction is met.

8.3   The Semantics of Applying Abstraction

There is one major advantage of properly asserting abstraction definitions with pre- and postconditions. When calling a properly asserted abstraction, the pre- and postconditions for the call are already known, at least in form. The abstraction interface really defines the abstraction's semantics. When calling the abstraction, the programmer must first ensure that, at the time of the call, the *actual* parameters will satisfy the abstraction's precondition – i.e., substitute each actual parameter for its corresponding formal parameter in the precondition and see if the resulting condition is satisfied by the pre-state. That's a lot to say! Before applying this principle, we will work through the following example, which determines the interface for a new abstraction.

Example 18 – Abstractions for data input
▼

> Suppose that you need an abstraction that will input an integer value that is guaranteed to be greater than or equal to some specified lower bound. The following call would seem to match what we want:[2]

---

[2]You might wonder why there is an identify condition in the postcondition – Persuasive Principle 1 says these should be suppressed. But in this case, if we suppress the identify condition, we can't tell if the value of `Low` might change. The intention of the interface is that `Low` not change.

```
int Bound, V;
...
// Assert: Low has a value
GetBoundedLow(Low, V);
// Assert: V >= Low AND Low == (pre)Low
...
```

But does this say enough? We know that the value will come from the input stream, but what if the first value the user enters is too small? While these assertions say what we expect to get back from the abstraction, they say nothing about any intention for dealing with faulty input.

The idea, of course, is that GetBoundedLow will take the first input value and return it *if* that value is greater than or equal to the bound value; if the input value is less than the bound, then another value will be read. In fact, the abstraction will repeatedly prompt and read a value until a valid entry is made. This means, for purposes of writing an interface, that we should think of the input stream as containing a sequence of input values (of arbitrary length) where all but the last are less than the bound value.[3] We can describe this with the following condition:

```
input stream == <v1,...,vn,v,...> AND
v1 < Low AND ... AND vn < Low     AND
v >= Low
```

This condition describes input stream before the call to GetBoundedLow. After the call we expect to see that the value of V is v, the initial values have been removed from input stream, and the value of the bound Low has not changed. We can reassert the call to GetBoundedLow as follows:

```
int Bound, Value;
...
// Assert: Low has a value                           AND
//         input stream == <v1,...,vn,v,...> AND
//         v1 < Low AND ... AND vn < Low     AND
//         v >= Low
GetBoundedLow(Low, Value);
// Assert: input stream == <...> AND
//         Value == v                AND
//         Value >= Low              AND
//         Low == (pre)Low
...
```

---

[3]This, of course, assumes that it is the first acceptable value we want returned – it could be the second or third.

Now, admittedly this is a lot to write down, but it is easy to understand. The abstraction interface would be written as follows:

```
void GetBoundedLow(int Low, int & V) {
     // Pre:  Low has a value                       AND
     //       input stream == <v1,...,vn,v,...> AND
     //       v1 < Low AND ... AND vn < Low       AND
     //       v >= Low
     // Post: input stream == <...> AND
     //       (out)V == v               AND
     //       (out)V >= (in)Low        AND
     //       (out)Low == (in)Low
```

▲

With this new abstraction interface in hand, suppose that we require a program that will input two integer values and then display the quotient and remainder which result when the first input value is divided by the second. The
following segment of code would seem to do the job:

```
int A, B, Quot, Rem;
...
cout << "Enter two integer values: ";
cin  >> A >> B;

QuotRem (A, B, Quot, Rem);

cout << A << "/" << B << " = "
     << Quot << " + " << Rem << "/" << B << endl;
```

But if the user makes a mistake and enters a negative value for A or B, the call
to QuotRem won't work as expected. Of course, the problem here is that we
have ignored the precondition for QuotRem.

We have just looked at an abstraction GetBoundedLow, which can help with
this problem. Since GetBoundedLow guarantees that it will return a positive
value in its actual parameter, we could use the following code:

```
int A, B, Quot, Rem;
...
// Assert: 0 is a value                       AND
//         input stream == <v1,...,vn,v,...> AND
//         v1 < 0 AND ... AND vn < 0           AND
//         v >= 0
GetBoundedLow(0, A);
// Assert: input stream == <...> AND
//         A == v               AND
//         A >= 0
```

```
// Assert: 1 is a value                         AND
//         input stream == <v1,...,vn,v,...> AND
//         v1 < 1 AND ... AND vn < 1           AND
//         v >= 1
GetBoundedLow(1, B);
// Assert: input stream == <...> AND
//         B == v                   AND
//         B >= 1

// Assert: A >= 0 AND B >= 1
QuotRem (A, B, Quot, Rem);
// Assert: A == Quot*B + Rem AND
//         0 <= Rem < B

cout << A << "/" << B << " = "
     << Quot << " + " << Rem << "/" << B << endl;
```

Though this is a simple segment of code, it is important to see that each assertion follows from the semantics of either one of the abstractions or of sequential execution. The code carries in its text evidence of its own correctness, and someone familiar with this technique should be persuaded that it is correct.

Being More Persuasive

The one criticism of the code above might be that it is difficult to see the code for the assertions. This is a problem with using the persuasive style – how can we bring out the essential semantics without getting bogged down in a forest of assertions? We can highlight a few important principles to remember about abstraction and persuasive programming:

1. It is important to provide each abstraction with an interface (pre- and postconditions) that is as complete as possible.

2. At each call to an abstraction it is important to state the interface in the state local to the call. This is an important reminder of what is expected before the call is made and of what is known of the state when the abstraction returns.

3. Those parts of the abstraction interface which are not relevant (a judgment call!) to the call's environment should be left out. After all, those details will be in the interface and can be referenced there.

The example above is a good one to consider in the light of these principles. In keeping with the first principle we have developed and included complete interfaces for the abstractions QuotRem and GetBoundedLow (see Examples 17 and 18). Also, in keeping with the second principle, we have included the interfaces of these abstractions set in the context of the calls. But we also see that the assertions associated with the calls to `GetBoundedLow` take up considerably more lines than does the actual code of the example. You might even say that the assertions make understanding what is going on more difficult. In keeping with the third principle, we should look carefully at each call and convince ourselves that all components of the assertions are relevant to the context of the calls. In the case of `GetBoundedLow`, understanding what happens to the input stream is not critical – knowing bounds on the values for A and B is critical. So leaving out the parts of those assertions relating to the input stream we arrive at the following equivalent code segment. The result is more in keeping with the persuasive style:

```
int A, B, Quot, Rem;
...
GetBoundedLow(0, A);
// Assert: A >= 0

GetBoundedLow(1, B);
// Assert: B >= 1

// Assert: A >= 0 AND B > 0
QuotRem (A, B, Quot, Rem);
// Assert: A == Quot*B + Rem AND
//            0 <= Rem < B

cout << A << "/" << B << " = "
     << Quot << " + " << Rem << "/" << B << endl;
```

It is important to notice that we really lose nothing by going to this less-detailed code. The earlier analysis we did was important in order to arrive at the fully asserted version – without that analysis we wouldn't know that the abbreviated version was reasonable. Also, the fully asserted version is easily reconstructed by including the full interface for `GetBoundedLow` at each call.

8.4 Inherent Semantics

The purpose of the abstraction pre- and postconditions is to define the intended semantics of the abstraction. But it is the code associated with the abstraction which determines what the abstraction actually does. The abstraction designer must ensure that the abstraction's inherent semantics matches the abstraction's intended semantics. This is really no different from the job of a program designer, who must design a program which will function as the user (customer) expects. In this section we will look at how to determine the inherent semantics and how it relates to the intended semantics.

A rather obvious initial question is which comes first, the intended or the inherent semantics? If the inherent semantics is determined first, that means that the programmer has decided to turn a particular segment of code into an abstraction. In this case, the intended semantics (the abstraction pre- and postconditions) are determined directly from the inherent semantics. It is more often the case, however, that abstractions are determined during the design process and result from looking at program activity at a more abstract level. In this case the intended semantics will be determined first – then an appropriate segment of code must be designed with inherent semantics that are the same as the intended semantics.

Our interest here is not how to design a correct algorithm knowing the intended semantics. That is a more advanced topic and will be addressed in a later lesson. We are interested in how to determine the inherent semantics of an abstraction and how to relate it to the intended semantics. We hope that what we discover will help you become an effective abstraction designer.

Before we look at some examples let's review the structure of an abstraction definition and highlight some characteristics that are important to the inherent semantics. Each abstraction definition consists of three basic components: a parameter list, local variable definitions, and a code segment. These three components determine a local environment which, when the abstraction is called, (temporarily) replaces the calling environment. This abstraction environment consists of the parameters, any local variables, and the program counter.[4]

Determining the inherent semantics of an abstraction is really quite straightforward. The abstraction precondition is a condition we are to assume will be satisfied by the input parameters – since these parameters are part of the abstraction's runtime environment, this precondition serves as the abstraction code segment's precondition. Working from the precondition and using techniques we have learned in previous lessons based on the semantics of the various simple statements and control structures, we work our way through the code segment and determine a postcondition for the segment. The derived postcondition will be written in terms of the local environment, i.e., the local variables and formal parameters of the abstraction definition. We know that when the abstraction returns, the local variables will cease to exist, so it is important to determine a condition that involves only the parameters. But there's more. Of the parameters, only the output parameters convey results back to the calling environment – values of the input parameters will be lost along with those of the local variables. So the final postcondition must reference only the output parameters and the original values of the input parameters. The hope, of course, is that this new condition will match the abstraction postcondition, indicating that the abstraction definition is correct.

The following examples will illustrate the points made concerning the inherent semantics and the way it can be determined. Keep in mind while working through these examples that there are three levels at which the intended and inherent semantics can be addressed. At the first level we start with an abstraction definition with intended semantics and derive the inherent semantics from the abstractions code segment. At the second level we start with the intended

---

[4]We are ignoring here the problem of global components to the environment. This problem is addressed in Lesson 10.

semantics and use our intuition and understanding of imperative semantics to generate a code segment with inherent semantics that are the same as the abstraction postcondition. In this case we generate the code segment sequentially, from first statement to last. The third level is the most formal and beyond the scope of this text. As in the previous case, we are given the intended semantics. But here we start with the abstraction postcondition and formally work backwards generating statements and preconditions: the goal is to generate the abstraction precondition. The examples illustrate the first level. With first-level practice you should be able to transition naturally to the second.

8.5   Functional Abstraction

From a definitional point of view, functional and procedural abstractions are quite similar. Both specify a list of formal parameters and a segment of code. The major differences are:

1. A functional abstraction specifies a (non-void) return type.

2. A specific return value is specified in the code segment. In C^{++} the return value is specified with the **return** statement.

Another difference, which students are usually taught in introductory programming courses, is the requirement that a functional abstraction returns only a single value. This would imply that a functional abstraction should not allow reference parameters in its formal parameter list. While this style is often promoted, most programming languages, including C^{++}, do not prohibit reference parameters in functional abstractions.

   Defining the interface for a functional abstraction, then, is very similar to defining one for a procedural abstraction – the only difference should be in specifying the return value. This is easily done by allowing a **return** clause in the postcondition. For example, we might want to convert the procedural abstraction `GetBoundedLow` to a functional abstraction. The following interface specifies the new form:

```
void GetBoundedLow(int Low) {
     // Pre:  Low has a value                      AND
     //       input stream == <v1,...,vn,v,...> AND
     //       v1 < Low AND ... AND vn < Low       AND
     //       v >= Low
     // Post: input stream == <...> AND
     //       return v
```

Notice that in the new form there is no need for the second formal parameter.

   A call to a functional abstraction can appear anywhere an expression can appear. This makes asserting such a call a bit troublesome. Here are a couple of examples of asserting calls to functional abstractions.

Example 19 – Calling a functional abstraction
▼

As a first example of asserting a functional abstraction call, we will reassert the segment of code from the end of the previous section, but making use of the functional version of `GetBoundedLow` rather than the procedural version.

```
int A, B, Quot, Rem;
...
A = GetBoundedLow(0);
// Assert: A >= 0

B = GetBoundedLow(1);
// Assert: B >= 1

// Assert: A >= 0 AND B > 0
QuotRem (A, B, Quot, Rem);
// Assert: A == Quot*B + Rem AND
//             0 <= Rem < B

cout << A << "/" << B << " = "
     << Quot << " + " << Rem << "/" << B << endl;
```

In this code the call to `GetBoundedLow` becomes the expression on the right of an assignment. Since we know that the value returned is not less than the value of the one actual parameter, we can state that the value of A or B has the same relationship after the assignment is made. This is a common way of calling a functional abstraction and, in this case, asserting the call is easy.

▲

Example 20 – Expressions with multiple abstraction calls
▼

One messy problem is an expression which contains several abstraction calls. Presumably we want to be able to assert the precondition for each of the calls – but how can we approach the problem?

```
choices = fact(n) / (fact(m) * fact(n-m))
```

In order to properly specify a precondition we must take into account each of the three abstraction calls which occur in the expression on the right.

What we want to remember is that persuasive programming is about being convincing. One approach is to introduce three new assignment statements, one to determine the value of each abstraction call.

In this way we can handle the precondition for each call separately. This approach might yield the following asserted code segment:

```
choices = fact(n) /(fact(m) * fact(n-m))
```

On the other hand, if the level of detail in the previous segment is not really needed, then we can combine the preconditions into one precondition and forget about computing intermediate values. We could use the following notation in this case:

```
// Assert: n >= 0        AND      -- fact(n)
//           m >= 0        AND      -- fact(m)
//          (n-m) >= 0     AND      -- fact(n-m)
//          fact(n-m) > 0
choices = fact(n) * fact(m)/fact(n-m)
// choices == n choose m
```

We could, of course, replace the three assertions lines as follows:

```
// Assert: 0 <= m <= n
choices = fact(n) / (fact(m) * fact(n-m))
// choices == n choose m
```

But the connection between this one relationship and the three abstraction calls is not as clear as the three-line assertion above. The first attempt seems more persuasive.

▲

Lesson 9

Are You Persuaded?

In the preceding three lessons we have focused on representing the semantics of the three high-level statement types: abstraction, selection, and repetition, but we have not considered these statements types in combination. In this lesson we will remedy this situation by investigating an example that uses all the standard statement types. The example focuses on a repetition statement whose body includes both a selection statement and an abstraction call.

9.1   The Problem – Finding the Largest Input Value

The following segment of code has been supplied complete with assertions that claim to describe the segment's semantics.

```
// Assert: input stream is <v1,...,vn,0> AND
//         v1 > 0,..., vn > 0
int Val;
Hi = 0;
GetBoundedLow(0, Val);
while (Val > 0) {
     if (Val > Hi)
         Hi = Val;
     GetBoundedLow(0, Val);
}
// Assert: input stream is <> AND
//         Hi is the largest of v1,...,vn,0
```

Are you persuaded? Our job in this section is to give a persuasive argument, in the form of appropriately asserted code, that the segment satisfies the claim.

121

9.2   Understanding the Assertions

Before we start analyzing the code segment, it is a good idea to make sure that we have a clear understanding of what the accompanying assertions say.

```
// Assert: input stream is <v1,...,vn,0> AND
//         v1 > 0,..., vn > 0
 .
 .
 .

// Assert: input stream is <> AND
//         Hi is the largest of v1,...,vn
```

The first assertion specifies the initial status of the input stream: the stream will contain a sequence of positive values followed by a zero. The one thing which isn't clear from this assertion is whether the sequence can be empty – i.e., that the input stream has only zero on it. We will keep this ambiguity in mind as we continue.

The second assertion indicates that the input stream is empty – apparently the code will read all the values including the zero – and that the variable Hi is the largest of the input values. More particularly, it must be the case that the value of Hi is the same as one of the input values and is greater than or equal to *all* the input values. So we can rewrite the second assertion more formally as follows:

```
// Assert: input stream is <> AND
//         (Hi == v1 OR  ... OR  Hi == vn) AND
//         (Hi >= v1 AND ... AND Hi >= vn)
```

While this new assertion is more formal, it is not necessarily a better choice from a persuasive programming point of view. However, when doing an analysis of a code segment such is this one, it is always important to know the formal equivalent for a verbal assertion.

9.3   Semantics of GetBoundedLow

Now that we understand the semantics we are to demonstrate, we can turn our attention to the code. We begin by looking at the one abstraction which is called in the code – GetBoundedLow. We saw this function first in Example 18 in Lesson 8. The interface of GetBoundedLow can be stated as follows:

```
void GetBoundedLow(int L, int & V)
  // pre:  L has a value AND
  //       input stream == <u1,...,un,u,s,...> AND
  //       u1<L AND ... AND un<L AND u >= L
  // post: input stream == <s,...> AND
  //       V == u                    AND
  //       V >= L
```

These semantics indicate that the function will read and ignore any number of invalid data values and then return as the value of V the first valid input value (i.e., the first one greater than or equal to L).

In the first assertion for our code segment there is no provision for invalid data values on the input stream. We can view this description as accurate – the code segment will not behave properly if there is invalid data in the input stream – or we can view the description as abstract and assume that, since GetBoundedLow will read and ignore such data, the possibility of invalid data is abstracted into each of the data stream values v1,...,vn,0. In that sense, it is only the value u in GetBoundedLow's precondition which is represented in the code segment's precondition. For our persuasive purposes we can use the following simplified interface for GetBoundedLow:

```
void GetBoundedLow(int L, int & V)
 // pre:  L has a value AND
 //       input stream == <u,s,...>
 // post: V == u AND
 //       input stream == <s,...>
```

9.4   Asserting the Loop

Now we turn our attention to the code segment. The segment is fundamentally a loop (with initialization) so we will use the three-step process illustrated in Lesson 7.

Step 1. *Determine a postcondition for the loop initialization.*

Asserting the loop initialization segment is almost straightforward, but there is one twist. When GetBoundedLow is called, since we don't know how many data values there are (how big n is), we only know that the return value of Val is greater than or equal to the lower bound 0. So we have to settle for the following postcondition for the loop initialization:

```
// Pre:  input stream is <v1,...,vn,0,...> AND
//       v1 > 0,..., vn > 0
int Val;

Hi = 0;
GetBoundedLow (0, Val);
// Assert: Hi == 0 AND Val >= 0
```

Step 2. *Determine a postcondition for the loop body.*

To determine a postcondition for the loop body we once more apply the technique of unwinding the loop – this strategy has worked well in earlier repetition examples, so it should help here. But we must be cautious because the loop body is not as simple as in the previous examples; the selection statement will make analysis more interesting.

As before, when writing down the unwinding we want to reflect the statements executed and the conditions that are satisfied at critical points in the execution. Here's the unwinding of the loop assuming there are three positive values on the input stream:

```
        // Assert: Hi == 0 AND Val == v1 > 0
a1      if (Val > Hi)
a2          Hi = Val;
a3      // A-1
a4      GetBoundedLow (0, Val);
a5      // A-1 AND Val >= 0 AND Val == v2

        // Assert: A-1 AND Val == v2 > 0
b1      if (Val > Hi)
b2          Hi = Val;
b3      // A-2
b4      GetBoundedLow (0, Val);
b5      // A-2 AND Val >= 0 AND Val == v3

        // Assert: A-2 AND Val == v3 > 0
c1      if (Val > Hi)
c2          Hi = Val;
c3      // A-3
c4      GetBoundedLow (0, Val);
c5      // A-3 AND Val >= 0 AND Val == 0
```

This sketch of the unwinding gives a basic structure but leaves crucial conditions unspecified (A-1, A-2, and A-3). We must tackle these one at a time in the hope that a pattern will emerge for the assertions at the three lines numbered 5. It is important that we remember that it is what happens to Hi that we are really interested in, and in the analysis which follows we will try to rephrase conditions to reflect this bias toward Hi.

A-1:

This first condition is relatively easy. We know that the initial value of Hi is zero and that the value of Val (v1) is positive, because the loop condition was true. This means that the if-condition (Val > Hi) on (line a1) must be true and the postcondition A-1 should be Hi == v1.

A-2:

On the second pass we can't count on the relative values of Val and Hi, so we must go with our standard pattern for a selection statement, which tells us that the lines b1 – b3 should look like:

```
b1  if (Val > Hi)
b2      Hi = Val;
b3  // (Val >  (pre)Hi AND Hi == Val)      OR
    // (Val <= (pre)Hi AND Hi == (pre)Hi)
```

This doesn't look too helpful! But if we take the two clauses of the `OR` separately and try to rephrase them in terms of `Hi` we can make progress. In the first clause, since `Hi` and `Val` are the same, we can replace `Val` with `Hi`. We can also replace `(pre)Hi` with its correct value `v1`.

```
// (Hi > v1 AND Hi == v2)
```

We can do a similar thing to the second clause, but this time we take advantage of the equality of `Hi` and `(pre)Hi`. The second clause becomes

```
// (v2 <= Hi AND Hi == v1)
```

After a bit of rearranging we get the following condition:

```
// (Hi >  v1 AND Hi == v2) OR
// (Hi >= v2 AND Hi == v1)
```

At this point, it is a good idea to recall what our program is supposed to do. It is to find the largest of the input values. Does our condition state this? Almost. But there is another modification which will make things clearer. First, recall that if `Hi` is *equal to* a value, then it is also *greater than or equal to* that same value. So we will add `Hi >= v2` to the first clause and `Hi >= v1` to the second. Also in each clause, we replace the ">" symbol with the ">=" symbol, which is a loss of information, but we don't really care which values `Hi` is greater than. From these modifications we get the following:

```
// (Hi >= v1 AND Hi >= v2 AND Hi == v2) OR
// (Hi >= v1 AND Hi >= v2 AND Hi == v1)
```

Finally, remember the distributive law for `AND`:

```
x AND (y OR z) <==> (x AND y) OR (x AND z)
```

If we take `(Hi >= v1 AND Hi >= v2)` for `x`, then the expression above is in the form of the right-hand side of the AND-distributive property. So we can replace the expression with the left-hand form and we get the following very useful looking condition to replace `A-2`:

```
// (Hi >= v1 AND Hi >= v2 AND (Hi == v2 OR Hi == v1))
```

A-3:

Now that we see the direction, we should be able to determine a condition for `A-3` in short order. Here is what we have to work with:

```
      // (Hi >= v1 AND Hi >= v2 AND
      //   (Hi == v2 OR Hi == v1))
      //     AND
      // Val == v3 > 0
   c1  if (Val > Hi)
   c2      Hi = Val;
   c3  // A-3
```

Once again we use the semantics of selection to determine A-3. Following the pattern we get the following condition:

```
// (Val >  (pre)Hi AND Hi == Val)      OR
// (Val <= (pre)Hi AND Hi == (pre)Hi)
```

Well, that looks familiar! We must remember that the value of (pre)Hi has properties guaranteed by the condition on line c1 and we use these properties to simplify A-3. We know in either case (Val > Hi or Val <= Hi) that after the selection statement Hi, either with its original value (pre)Hi or with the new value v3, will be greater or equal to v1, v2, and v3 and that Hi will still have one of the values v1 or v2, or it will have the new value v3. So the condition A-3 can be written as follows:

```
// ( (Hi >= v1 AND Hi >= v2 AND Hi >= v3) AND
//   (Hi == v1 OR  Hi == v2 OR  Hi == v3) )
```

This analysis gives us a general form which will work regardless of the number of positive input values. To make the assertion truly general we must make use of the (R) notation, which denotes the number of passes through the loop. Here is the general form which we have deduced for the asserted loop body:

```
if (Val > Hi)
    Hi = Val;


GetBoundedLow (0, Val);
// Assert: (Hi == v1 OR  ... OR  Hi == v(R)) AND
//         (Hi >= v1 AND ... AND Hi >= v(R)) AND
//          Val >= 0
```

You should recognize this as having the same form as we associated with the phrase "Hi is the largest of v1,...,v(R)" – see the earlier section titled *Understanding the Assertions*.

Step 3. *Determine a postcondition for the loop.*

Now we complete the task by determining the postcondition for the entire loop – and the code segment as well. This is almost straightforward. We would like to adopt the following condition as our postcondition:

```
Hi = 0;
GetBoundedLow (0, Val);
// Assert: Val >= 0 AND Hi == 0
while (Val > 0) {
      if (Val > Hi)
          Hi = Val;
      GetBoundedLow (0, Val);
}
// Assert: Val == 0 AND
//         Hi is the largest of v1,...,vn
```

The justification for replacing v(R) with vn, of course, is that when the loop terminates, (R) will have value equal to the number of passes through the loop – which equals the number of input values n.

But another problem returns. Is it possible for there to be an empty sequence? If the input sequence is empty, then the loop body is never entered and in this case the value of Hi will be zero. We can take care of this possibility and resolve the question of empty input sequence by adopting the following postcondition:

```
Hi = 0;
GetBoundedLow (0, Val);
// Assert: Val >= 0 AND Hi == 0

while (Val > 0) {
        if (Val > Hi)
            Hi = Val;

        GetBoundedLow (0, Val);
}
// Assert: Val == 0 AND
//         Hi is the largest of v1,...,vn
```

Notice that we have included the value zero. If there are no positive input values, then the value of Hi must be zero.

The final asserted form is as follows:

```
Hi = 0;
GetBoundedLow (0, Val);
// Assert: Val >= 0 AND Hi == 0

while (Val > 0) {
        if (Val > Hi)
            Hi = Val;

        GetBoundedLow (0, Val);
        // Assert: Val >= 0   AND
        //         Hi is the largest of v1,...,v(R)
}
// Assert: Val == 0 AND
//         Hi is the largest of v1,...,vn,0
```

Part III

Statement Semantics:
A Second Look

Lesson 10

Semantics and Data Abstraction

A data type is defined to be a set of data values along with a set of operations for manipulating the data. The data types we have seen so far (`int, float, bool`) are called *simple* or *atomic* types because their values have no structure – i.e., the values can't be separated into components. The other usual atomic types include `char`, where the values are the ASCII character codes, and the user-defined *enumerated types*, whose values are identifiers defined by the programmer. These simple data types are inspired by, and for the most part derived from, the sets of data values and operations that are supported by the computer processor.

When we talk about *abstract data types* we mean types in which each data value is a combination of values from other (already defined) data types and the operations are specifically designed for the particular sets of data values. The operations are defined using abstraction, which we have already looked at, but the structure of the data is described using a new language structure called a *type constructor*. From a persuasive programming perspective, three questions naturally arise:

1. How should we represent logical conditions on values of an abstract data type?

2. How do we describe the semantics of the operations associated with abstract data types?

3. Are there any new assertion-related structures which arise naturally from the use of abstract data types?

The last question anticipates a new application for state-based logical conditions. To give a hint of this new application, consider an abstract data type for fractions – each fraction value is comprised of two integer values — a numerator and a denominator. A global property we might want to guarantee for every

131

fraction value is that the denominator cannot be zero. Such a property is called a `type invariant`.

We will begin this lesson with a brief review of the three basic type constructors; i.e., for describing array types, record types, and classes. The second section addresses the first two questions above and introduces new logical structures, the *bounded universal quantifier* and the *bounded existential quantifier*. Section three gives examples applying the new logical structures to various data types. The fourth section illustrates the importance of the type invariant and how it affects the definition and implementation of an abstract data type.

10.1   A Brief Review

The data analyzed by computer programs comes in a great variety of forms. Geometric data can be in rectangular form, where each point is determined by a pair of distances from an origin, or in polar form, where each point is determined by a distance from an origin and a rotation through an angle (from a base line). An organization's personnel records can have a quite complex structure, with some data components present just for certain categories of employees. Other common abstract data types include lists, stacks, queues, trees, and graphs. The job of a programmer is to take the natural structure of the data for a problem and somehow describe that structure using the basic data types provided by the programming language.

Because the structure of data cannot be easily anticipated, modern programming languages have evolved to include mechanisms, called *type constructors*, for defining – constructing – new data types in terms of already defined data types. There are three primary constructors in common use – array, record, and class – and all three are implemented in C^{++}.

The Array Constructor

Defining: The *array* constructor is used to specify a homogeneous data type – one in which each data value is a fixed length sequence of data values, all of the same specified (already defined) base type. We call such a constructed type an *array type*.

An array variable X for which each value is a sequence of 20 integer values could be defined in C^{++} as follows:

```
int X[20];
```

The array type constructor is represented by the balanced square brackets, with the value 20 being a parameter to the constructor indicating the size of the array X – we call each value in this type an *integer array*.

Referencing: Each component of an array value can be referenced individually. An array names its components with a sequence of integer values beginning with 0. The following examples illustrate references to components of X as defined above:

```
X[4]            // 5th component in X
X[0]            // first component in X
X[I+1]          // evaluate I+1 and access
                //   the resulting position in X
```

In this last example, if "I+1" evaluates to less than 0 or greater than 19, the reference is considered to be an error.

The Record Constructor

Defining: The *record* constructor is used to specify a heterogeneous data type – one in which each data value is a fixed length collection of data values of (possibly) different but already defined types. We call such a constructed type a *record type* or, in the case of C^{++}-like languages, a *struct* type. We say that a record type is composed of *components*, each with a specified name and type.

A record variable for which there are two components, one whose value is a name and the other whose value is an age, might be denoted in C^{++} as follows:

```
struct {
        char Name[20];
        int     Age;
      } Person;
```

Notice that each component of the data's structure has an associated identifier.

Referencing: The *dot notation* is used to reference the components of a record value as illustrated here:

```
Person.Name        // the Name component of Person
Person.Age         // the Age component of Person
Person.Name[4]     // the 5th character in the
                   //   Name component of Person
```

Unlike the array type, there is no importance in the ordering of the components of a record.

The Class Constructor

Defining: The *class constructor* is a more abstract constructor than the other two. It is used to encapsulate not only the structure of data values, but also the operations (methods, in C^{++} parlance) allowed on the data.[1] We refer to such a constructed type as a *class* and the values of a class as *objects*. A simple class for implementing fractions might be defined in C^{++} as follows:

```
class fraction {
        int Numerator;
        int Denominator;

        fraction (int n, int d);
        void setFraction(int n, int d);
        void reduce();
        int  getNumerator();
        int  getDenominator();
}
```

Notice that, as in the record type, each data component of a class has an associated identifier and type. Each operation or method, on the other hand, is described by a more complex structure called a *signature*, which consists of the method name, return type, and the *type* of each formal parameter (parameter names are not required).

Referencing: Components of an object (variable of a class type) are referenced using the same dot notation described for the record type. The following examples illustrate such references:

```
fraction X(1,4);  // constructs a fraction value initialized
                  // with numerator 1 and denominator 4

int Y = X.getNumerator(); // assign the numerator of X to Y

// Assert: n and d have values
X.setFraction(n,d); // give X a new fraction value
                    //   based on n and d
```

---

[1]The **struct** type constructor of C^{++}, usually used for defining record types, can also be used to encapsulate operations and data like the class constructor. We will ignore this property of **struct**, since it is subsumed by the class constructor. In Java the record constructor has disappeared completely, having been replaced by the class structure.

10.2 New Logical Structures – Bounded Quantifiers

It is important to point out a basic difference in the nature of array values as opposed to record and class values. The record and class constructors provide a mechanism for encapsulating related data (and methods, in the case of the class), but this encapsulation implies nothing about any "algorithmic" association among the values of components. Array values, on the other hand, routinely have their components searched, sorted, and variously reshuffled and modified. This type of manipulation is possible because of the flexibility afforded by the component reference mechanism for array values. The next two sections will focus on what we must do to adapt persuasive programming to this algorithmic context of array values. We return to the record and class constructors in the last two sections of the Lesson.

When describing logical properties of data in an array there are two basic statement types that appear:

- A particular property is true for every data value in the array.

- There is at least one data value in the array for which a particular property holds.

In logical terms we call the first property *bounded universal*, since it is true for the universe of data values in the array, and the second property *bounded existential*, since it states the existence of a data value in the array with the particular property. The term *bounded* refers to the fact that a property holds for a particular array or part of an array, rather than for all arrays.

Bounded Universal Quantifier (BUQ)

Though we understand the description of bounded quantifiers given above, it is important to persuasive programming that we be more precise. When we want to say an array satisfies a bounded universal property, we are really only interested in those array elements that have been assigned values. This means that when stating a bounded universal property we should specify the index range over which the property holds. So we will usually make statements such as

> For every index value I ranging from zero to N, property P(I) is satisfied.

Or more succinctly,

> For I=0,...,N: P(I).

In this expression a new "pseudo variable" I is introduced and it is important to be clear on the extent of its scope – i.e., the range of the expression for which the name I can be used. For the bounded universal quantifier (BUQ) the scope of I extends to the end of the property P(I). The property P(I) is perhaps a bit mysterious. In fact it can be replaced by any logical expression based on the variable I. Here are a few examples:

> For I=0,...,N-1: A[I] > 0
> This simply says that every array value is positive – the property is "A[I] > 0."

> For I=0,...,N-2: A[I] ≤ A[I+1]
> This says that the elements in the array A are in increasing order – the property is "A[I] ≤ A[I+1]."

> For I=0,...,K: For J=N,...,M: A[I][J] < B[I][J]
> This says that for each value of I ranging from 0 to M, A[I][J] < B[I][J] is true for every value of J ranging from N to M.

In this last example notice that the expression associated with the pseudo variable I contains a BUQ. The structure of this nested BUQ has the same characteristics as nested `for` statements in C^{++}.

Bounded Existential Quantifier (BEQ)

Similarly we can specify an index range in which a bounded existential property holds:

> There is an index value I such that I is between zero and N and property P(I) is satisfied.

Or more succinctly,

> There is I: 0 ≤ I ≤ N AND P(I).

Here are a few examples:

> There is I: 0 <= I <= N AND (A[I] == 0)
> This states that there is at least one position in the array A for which the value is zero.

> There is I: 0 <= I <= N AND (A[I] != A[0])
> This states that there is at least one position in the array A for which the value is different from the value at A[0] – the first position in A.

> There is I: 0 < I < N AND For J=0,...,M: A[I][J] == T
> This states that there is a particular row in the array A for which every value equals the value of T.

An interesting relationship holds between these specialized expressions. The logical negation of a bounded universal property is a bounded existential property, and vice versa. The rules are as follows – we use the symbol ⟺ to indicate that two expressions are equivalent.

```
NOT(For I=0 to N: P(I))  ⟺  There is I: 0 ≤ I ≤ N AND (NOT P)
```

```
NOT (There is I: 0 ≤ I ≤ N AND P(I))  ⟺  For I=0 to N: NOT P
```

Those statements can sound a bit odd, so here are a couple of examples to illustrate the equivalences:

```
NOT (For I=0 to N-1:  A[I] > 0)  ⟺
There is I: 0 ≤ I ≤ N-1 AND (A[I] ≤ 0)
```

```
NOT (There is I: 0 ≤ I ≤ N AND (A[I] != A[0]))  ⟺
For I=0 to N: A[I] == A[0]
```

By being more precise about the index range over which a property is to hold, it will often be the case that an appropriately structured assertion (post-condition) will bear a close resemblance to an algorithm which will guarantee the assertion will hold. This is a pleasant surprise which comes with the use of these more complex logical structures.

10.3 Applying Bounded Quantifiers

Suppose we are working on a program in which one part maintains a list of values in an array – for simplicity we will assume that the values in the list are integers and that there is a variable for maintaining the length of the list. The structure of the list can be described by the following declarations:

```
// Assert: SIZE > 0
int L[SIZE];
int      length = 0;
```

There are many operations we may wish to implement for this list structure – AddElement, DeleteAt, Display, Sort, or Search. The semantics of each of these operations can be best described making use of the bounded quantifiers just introduced. We will focus on the operation AddElement to see how the new quantifiers can be applied in describing the operation's interface.

The action we expect AddElement to perform is to add an element to L as long as there is room in the array for the new element. Here is an incomplete interface for the operation:

```
void AddElement(int value, int & len, int L[]) {
    // Pre:  ???
    // Post: ???

    L[len] = value;
    len = len + 1;
}
```

We want to supply the pre- and postconditions for `AddElement`. The pre-condition is relatively straightforward: the value of `len` must be less than the maximum capacity of the array, and the array should already have values in its first `len` positions. The first condition can be simply stated as "`len < SIZE`". But the second condition requires the BUQ in order to say that all the array positions (up to `len-1`) have values. We can write the precondition as follows:

```
// Pre:  len < SIZE AND
//       For I=0 to len-1: L[I] has a value
```

We make no claim about the values in the other positions in L.

What about the postcondition? If we add the element to the end of the current sequence of values in L, then (out)L will be the same as (in)L in the first `len` positions, i.e., positions 0...`len-1`, and have the new value at position `len`. In addition, the value of `len` is increased by one. The following postcondition works:

```
// Post: For I=0 to (in)len-1: (out)L[I] == (in)L[I] AND
//       (out)L[len] == value                         AND
//       (out)len == (in)len+1
```

It is important to notice how the postcondition compares to the statements in the body of `AddElement`'s definition. The first line of the postcondition states that the initial part of the list remains unchanged – no code was necessary to make this true. The second two lines mimic the two code lines in the implementation. If we had this specification first, we would know exactly what code to write. The fully asserted code would look as follows:

```
void AddElement(int value, int & len, int L[]) {
    // Pre:  len < SIZE AND
    //       For I=0 to len-1: L[I] has a value
    // Post: For I=0 to (in)len-1: (out)L[I] == (in)L[I] AND
    //       (out)L[len] == value                         AND
    //       (out)len == (in)len+1

    L[len] = value;
    len = len + 1;
}
```

Adding an Element in the Middle

To emphasize that repetition code can be easily deduced from a postcondition with a BUQ, we look at the same problem with a slight alteration: We supply an additional parameter that specifies the position in the list where the new value is to be inserted. Rather than looking at implementation first, let's start with the interface. A call to the modified `AddElement` should look like this:

```
AddElement(v, position, len, L)
```

where v is the value to be added at `position` in the array L with `len` elements. We look at the precondition first. This should be the same as before with the exception that the value of `position` had better be appropriate as an insertion point – this means anywhere from position 0 up to the first position following the current list, i.e., the value of `len`, so the following precondition seems appropriate:

```
// Pre:  len < SIZE                             AND
//       For I=0 to len-1: L[I] has a value AND
//       0 <= position <= len
```

Now the fun part. How should we describe the status of the list when the call returns? What will be different from the previous case? The returned list should be the same as the original list up to the point of insertion, then the rest of the original list should be offset by one in the final list starting one position past the insertion point. We can state this as follows:

```
// Post: For I=0 to position-1:
//              (out)L[I] == (in)L[I]
//           AND
//        For I=position+1 to (in)len:
//              (out)L[I] == (in)L[I-1]
//           AND
//        (out)L[position] == value
//           AND
//        (out)len == (in)len+1
```

This postcondition is interesting because it tells us precisely what code we need for the body of `AddElement`.

```
for (I=position+1; I <= len; I++) {
    L[I] = L[I-1];
}
L[position] = value;
len = len + 1;
```

These C^{++} statements come almost for free out of the postcondition. The key is the fact that the C^{++} `for` statement translates easily from the BUQ. This is a very nice characteristic of many operations performed on arrays.

Three Examples

Though we have introduced the bounded quantifiers in the context of arrays, it turns out that these logical structures are useful in many situations. In fact, the bounded universal quantifier would have been useful in earlier lessons. The following examples illustrate this point.

Example 21 – The integer is prime

▼

Here is an example that involves just a simple value – an integer value. We want to write a condition that is true exactly when the value is prime. What does this mean for an integer variable X? It means that

- X >= 2 and
- if 2 <= I < X, the value I doesn't divide X evenly, i.e., X mod I != 0.

This second point states a condition which must be true for all values in a range, which implies the use of a BUQ. The following condition is appropriate:

```
X >= 2 AND
For I = 2,...,X-1: X mod I != 0
```

Notice that this condition is true when X == 2 because the For clause specifies an empty interval. We can actually do better. When checking to see if a number is prime we needn't check any value greater than the square root[2] of X – using this bound we can adopt the following condition:

```
X >= 2 AND
For I = 2,...,sqrt(X): X mod I != 0
```

One advantage of rewriting the condition is that it implies a more efficient algorithm.

▲

Example 22 – Data input revisited

▼

In Example 18 in Lesson 8.3 we developed the following interface for GetBoundedLow, which is supposed to return the first input value that meets or exceeds a specified lower bound:

```
void GetBoundedLow(int Low, int & V) {
    // Pre:  Low has a value                        AND
    //       input stream == <v1,...,vn,v,...> AND
    //       v1 < Low AND ... AND vn < Low      AND
    //       vn >= Low
    // Post: input stream == <...> AND
    //       (out)V == v                AND
    //       (out)V >= (in)Low
```

---

[2]Remember that if a is a factor of X and $a > \sqrt{X}$, then there must be another factor of X, $X = a * b$, and $b < \sqrt{X}$. The algorithm described will find b rather than a if $\sqrt{X}$ is used as the bound.

When we look at this interface we see the third line of the precondition, which looks like a universal statement. In fact, we can restate
that precondition using the BUQ as follows:

```
void GetBoundedLow(int Low, int & V) {
      // Pre:  Low has a value                          AND
      //       input stream == <v1,...,vn,v,...> AND
      //       For I=1,...,n: vI < Low               AND
      //       v >= Low
      // Post: input stream == <...> AND
      //       (out)V == v              AND
      //       (out)V >= (in)Low
```

In Example 7.4 we looked at a similar input problem, where the value
returned is bounded above *and* below. Here is the precondition used
in that example:

```
// Pre:  Low <= Hi
//           AND
//       input stream == <v1,...,vn>
//           AND
//       ((v1 < Low OR v1 > Hi) AND
//           ...               AND
//        (v(n-1) < Low OR v(n-1) > Hi))
//           AND
//       (Low <= vn <= Hi)
```

Here the BUQ can also be useful. We can rewrite the third line of
the precondition and get the following precondition:

```
// Pre:  Low <= Hi                               AND
//       input stream == <v1,...,vn>             AND
//       For I=1,...,(n-1): (vI < Low OR vI > Hi) AND
//       (Low <= vn <= Hi)
```

▲

The previous examples have all made use of the BUQ. There is one important notational device that is used repeatedly. In writing assertions we must
make use of the same keyboard characters used in writing program statements.
In the examples above we have used v1 where, with a more sophisticated display
environment, we might otherwise have written v_1 – i.e., the 1 is a subscript. Following a name immediately with a number is a convenient notation to substitute
for subscripting. But this is not without problems. In the examples above we
also use expressions involving variable-like names to represent subscripts. For
example, vn is meant to denote the nth element in the sequence of values and
v(n-1) denotes the "n minus first" element in the sequence. This subscript
notation can become clumsy in certain complex situations, but care in layout
of the expressions can ease readability problems.

Example 23 – Finding the largest value

▼

In Lesson 9.1 we looked at code for finding the largest value in an input stream. We began with the following interface for the abstraction `GetLargest`:

```
void GetLargest (int &Hi) {
      // Pre:  input stream is <v1, v2, ..., vn, 0> AND
      //       v1 > 0, ..., vn > 0
      // Post: input stream is <empty>              AND
      //       (out)Hi is the largest of v1,...,vn
```

In light of what we have seen in previous examples in this lesson, we should conclude that this interface could be improved. The second line of the precondition is a universal statement, but the second line of the postcondition sounds like an existential statement. How should these two lines be rewritten? The line in the precondition is easy because we have seen several examples just like it in the examples above. We can rewrite as follows:

```
//          For I=1,...,n: vI > 0
```

Now, what about the second line of the postcondition? What we discovered in the example in Lesson 9.1 is that there are really two statements implied here. First, that `Hi` is greater than or equal to all the values, a universal property, *and* that it is equal to at least one of them, an existential property. These can easily be restated as follows:

```
void GetLargest (int &Hi) {
      // Pre:  input stream is <v1, v2, ..., vn, 0>
      //          AND
      //          For I=1,...,n: vI > 0
      // Post: input stream is <empty>
      //          AND
      //          There is I: 1 <= I <= n AND (out)Hi == vI
      //          AND
      //          For I=1,...,n: (out)Hi >= vI
```

▲

10.4   The Data Invariant

There is a very important concept not to be missed in this discussion of data abstraction. A *data invariant* is a property associated with a data type. Every value of the type should satisfy the data invariant. By formalizing the data invariant the programmer makes explicit properties which the program code must maintain.

The significance of the data invariant is actually to the operations or methods associated with the type or class. This is because in stating a data invariant, the programmer is also stating a requirement that any operation on a variable of the type maintain the invariant on that variable.

The fraction Type

As a simple example consider the following record-based definition for a fraction type (we earlier saw a class-based definition for a fraction type):

```
fraction struct {
            int Num;
            int Den;
        }
```

As far as C^{++} is concerned, this definition indicates that every pair of integer values associated with Num and Den defines a value of type **fraction**. But we know logically that this cannot be; in particular, only pairs for which Den is not zero should qualify as fraction values. C^{++} does not provide a mechanism for specifying or enforcing this restriction. Instead, it is up to the programmer to use values of type **fraction** in an appropriate way. In this case we can augment the definition of **fraction** by including a comment stating the data invariant. Notice that the type name is included in the comment.

```
fraction struct {
            int Num;
            int Den;
        }
// fraction invariant: Den != 0
```

Of course, there may be more restrictions. For example, it would be convenient if we know which component of **fraction** carries the sign of the fraction. If we want the sign to be carried by the numerator, then we can write the invariant as follows:

```
fraction struct {
            int Num;
            int Den;
        }
// fraction invariant: Den > 0
```

The fact that no restriction is applied to Num means that it can take any value of its type.

One other restriction we might want to enforce is that the component values of every fraction value be reduced to lowest terms – in other words, there is no value which divides both the numerator and denominator other than one. Here is a final definition for the fraction type incorporating this last restriction:

```
fraction struct {
            int Num;
            int Den;
        }
// fraction invariant:
//          Den > 0 AND
//          ( (Num == 0 AND Den == 1) OR
//            (Num != 0 AND
//              For I=2,...,Den-1:
//                Den % I != 0 OR Num % I != 0) )
```

To see how the invariant would affect operation implementation, consider the implementations of two operations for the following abbreviated fraction class:

```
fraction class {
// fraction invariant:
//          Den > 0 AND
//          ( (Num == 0 AND Den == 1) OR
//            (Num != 0 AND
//              For I=2,...,Den-1:
//                Den % I != 0 OR Num % I != 0) )
    int Num;
    int Den;

    fraction();
    void setFraction(int n, int d);
    void addTo(fraction f);

    int  gcd(int n, int m);
}
```

In implementing each operation we must be sure to leave the method code knowing that the invariant is once again true. Notice it doesn't matter if the invariant becomes false during execution of the method. The invariant only requires that the invariant hold before and after a method's execution.

```
fraction::fraction() {
    // Pre:  none
    // Post: Num == 0 AND Den == 1
    //       invariant is maintained
    Num = 0; Den = 1;
}
```

```
void fraction::setFraction(int n, int d) {
   // Pre:  n has values AND d != 0
   // Post: (out)Num*d == (out)Den*n AND
   //          invariant is maintained

   if (n == 0) { Num = 0; Den = 1; }
   else { x = gcd(n,m);
          Num = n/x;
          Den = d/x;
          if (Den < 0) { Num = (-1)*Num; Den = (-1)*Den; }
   }
}


void fraction::addTo(fraction f) {
   // Pre:  f has a value
   // Post: (out)Num*(in)Den*f.Den ==
   //            (out)Den*(f.Num*(in)Den + f.Den*(in)Num)
   //          AND
   //          invariant is maintained

   setFraction(f.Num*Den + f.Den*Num ,Den*f.Den);
}
```

The list Type

Another interesting example comes from the realm of lists. Though you may think of a list as represented by an array of values, most lists are a bit more. Since lists are usually dynamic (changing in size) it is usual to implement a list with a pair of data values – an array to hold the values and an integer variable to indicate the length of the list. The following provides a convenient way to define a list type:

```
intList struct {
            int List[MaxLength];
            int NumEntries;
        }
```

As with the type fraction we should think of any important properties this type should be guaranteed to have. There are a few. The most important invariant for this type is that the NumEntries component always accurately reflect the number of values stored in the List component. More subtly, it is usually assumed that the values are stored in consecutive locations starting at index zero.

```
intList struct {
          int List[MaxLength];
          int NumEntries;
     }
// intList invariant: 0 <= NumEntries <= MaxLength AND
//                     For I=0,...,NumEntries-1:
//                        List[I] has a value
```

The invariant is an important component of any abstract data type. But stating the invariant is not enough. It is up to the programmer to insure that every operation on values of the type maintains the invariant.

Lesson 11

More on Selection

In Lesson 6 we looked at the semantics of selection statements where only one selection condition was allowed. In this lesson we will remove that restriction and consider selection problems which involve more than one condition. By applying the techniques of Lesson 6, we will derive a general asserted form which can be used for asserting any selection statement. We will also discuss the C^{++} `switch` statement and introduce an alternative form for expressing selection semantics based on logical implication.

11.1 n-way Selection – An Overview

We begin with a simple but classic example. We want to be able to print the number of real roots for any second-degree polynomial $Ax^2 + Bx + C$. We know that the value of the discriminant of the polynomial, $B^2 - 4AC$, determines the number of roots, so the following chart can be used to guide us in the design of our code segment:

$B^2 - 4AC$	# roots	print this
> 0	2	"There are 2 real roots."
$== 0$	1	"There is 1 real root."
< 0	0	"There are no real roots."

Because there are three conditions which can be met, we call this a three-way selection problem. If you were asked to invent a new kind of programming statement that would be convenient for implementing solutions to such problems, you might come up with the following **doone** statement:

```
D = B*B - 4*A*C;
doone {
   (D > 0)   : cout << "There are 2 real roots." << endl;
   (D == 0)  : cout << "There is 1 real root." << endl;
   (D < 0)   : cout << "There are no real roots." << endl;
}
```

This syntax captures what we intuitively think three-way selection should be – the key-word `doone` is to be read "do one."

An n-way selection problem can be characterized as a sequence of n disjoint conditions, each paired with a specific action which is to be carried out if the condition is true. When we execute an n-way selection statement, in the form of the `doone` statement above, for example, the conditions are evaluated in sequence until one is encountered which evaluates to `true`: the corresponding code segment is then executed. If all the conditions evaluate to `false` then no action is taken. The *with-default* version of n-way selection has an extra code segment specified which is executed if all the conditions evaluate to `false`,[1] Remember, since the conditions are disjoint, at most one of the conditions can evaluate to true.

While n-way selection is quite common in programming, C^{++} does not have a specific n-way selection statement. Instead, in C^{++} n-way selection is implemented using one-way selection (i.e., the if-then-else construction). The following C^{++} segment implements the "number of roots" problem described above:

```
// Assert: D == B*B - 4*A*C

if (D > 0)
    cout << "Ax^2 + Bx + C has two roots" << endl;
else if (D == 0)
        cout << "Ax^2 + Bx + C has one root" << endl;
else if (D < 0)
        cout << "Ax^2 + Bx + C has no roots" << endl;
```

The execution pattern is easy to follow. If the first selection condition is true then the first output statement is executed. But if the condition evaluates to false, the default (else-part) code segment (a nested one-way selection) is executed. So if the first condition is false we immediately evaluate the second condition. If the second is true the second output statement is executed, but if it is false then the default, the third nested one-way selection, is executed, etc.

From this example it is easy to see the execution pattern for a C^{++} n-way selection statement. Evaluate the specified conditions in the order they appear until one is found which true: execute the code segment paired with the true condition and then ignore the rest of the statement. If all the conditions are evaluated and none is found to be true then the final default segment is executed if there is one; if there is no default then no action is taken.

You have probably noted that the final condition in this roots example is not necessary, since execution only reaches the third option if the value of D

---

[1] This is not the most general form of n-way selection. Dijkstra, in his well-known paper *Guarded Commands, Nondeterminacy and Formal Derivation of Programs* (E.W. Dijkstra, Communications of the ACM, Vol. 18 No. 8, pp. 453 – 457 1975) introduced the *guarded commands*, one of which generalizes n-way selection. When the guarded selection statement is executed *all* conditions are evaluated; if one or more conditions evaluates to `true`, then one of the conditions is selected and the corresponding code segment executed. If all conditions are false, then the statement fails – i.e., a runtime error occurs.

is negative – exactly the condition. So we can modify the statement to be a two-way selection with default.

```
// Assert: D == B*B - 4*A*C
if (D > 0) cout << "Ax^2 + Bx + C has two roots" << endl;
else if (D == 0) cout << "Ax^2 + Bx + C has 1 root" << endl;
else // Assert: D < 0
    cout << "Ax^2 + Bx + C has no roots" << endl;
```

Let's look at another illustration of *n*-way selection. Suppose that data are being collected to show the age distribution of customers visiting a shop. The following table defines the age categories and actions appropriate in a four-way selection statement:

Age	Category	Code Segment
5 - 12	Child	update `Children = Children + 1;`
13 - 19	Teenager	update `Teens = Teens + 1;`
20 - 25	Young Adult	update `YoungAdults = YoungAdults + 1;`
≥ 26	Adult	update `Adults = Adult + 1;`

The information in the table can easily be translated into the form of a C^{++} four-way selection. Notice that the code examines a variable `Customer`, which is assumed to hold the age of a customer, and updates the appropriate counter depending on the category to which the value of `Customer` belongs.

```
if (5 <= Customer && Customer <= 12)
    Children = Children + 1;
else if (Customer <= 19 && Customer >= 13)
    Teens = Teens + 1;
else if (Customer <= 25 && Customer >= 20)
    YoungAdults = YoungAdults + 1;
else if (Customer >= 26)
    Adult = Adult + 1;
```

It may appear that the order in which the conditions are checked makes a difference – but because the conditions are disjoint, the order doesn't matter.

If the value of `Customer` is obtained via input, then, by making use of the abstraction `GetBoundedLow`, we can simplify the code from a four-way selection without default to a three-way selection with default:

```
GetBoundedLow(5, Customer);
// Assert: Customer >= 5
if (5 <= Customer && Customer <= 12)
    Children = Children + 1;
else if (Customer <= 19 && Customer >= 13)
    Teens = Teens + 1;
else if (Customer <= 25 && Customer >= 20)
    YoungAdults = YoungAdults + 1;
else // Customer >= 26
    Adult = Adult + 1;
```

Why does this work? In the four-way version above, when the final `else` is reached, the previous three conditions are known to be false so the value of `Customer` doesn't fall in the intervals `[5,12]`, `[13,19]`, `[20,25]` – i.e., the value of `Customer` must be larger than 25 or it could be less than 4! What we have done here is make use of `GetBoundedLow` to guarantee that the value of `Customer` cannot be less than 4. This means that in the final `else`, there is no need to check if `Customer` is greater than or equal to 26, because those are the only possible values `Customer` can have. The final condition check becomes redundant and unnecessary.

When Conditions Are not Disjoint

Because of the way n-way selection is implemented in C^{++}, and in most other imperative languages as well, it is actually possible to implement a selection statement using non-disjoint conditions. This is easily illustrated using the age-classification problem just discussed. The following code segment is equivalent to the three-way selection above:

```
GetBoundedLow(5, Customer);
// Assert: Customer >= 5

if (Customer <= 12)
    Children = Children + 1;
else if (Customer <= 19)
    Teens = Teens + 1;
else if (Customer <= 25)
    YoungAdults = YoungAdults + 1;
else // Customer >= 26
    Adult = Adult + 1;
```

Let's consider carefully how execution of the first three-way selection progresses. If the first condition fails (i.e., evaluates to `false`), then when the second condition is evaluated, we already know that the value of `Customer` is greater than or equal to 13. This means we should not have to evaluate the "<= 12" condition again. Consequently, we can simplify the form of the three-way selection and gain some efficiency. Here is a more likely implementation of the age-classification selection statement:

```
GetBoundedLow(5, Customer);
// Assert: Customer >= 5

if (Customer <= 12)        // acceptance of initial assertion
                           // guarantees Customer >= 5
    Children = Children + 1;
else if (Customer <= 19)   // failure of previous condition
                           // guarantees that Customer >= 13
    Teens = Teens + 1;
```

```
else if (Customer <= 25)      // failure of previous condition
                              // guarantees that Customer >= 20
    YoungAdults = YoungAdults + 1;
else // Customer >= 26
    Adult = Adult + 1;
```

The comments after each if serve to justify the simplifications. Notice that, whereas the original selection conditions were all disjoint, this is no longer the case. The important thing to remember is that this simplification process can be reversed, making it possible to re-form the original disjoint conditions. It is the disjoint conditions that are central to the semantics of *n*-way selection.

11.2   Semantics of *n*-way Selection – Analysis

Since *n*-way selection statements are built from one-way selection statements, an understanding of the semantics of *n*-way selection should follow from our understanding of one-way selection semantics. We will use our three-way selection example above for our investigation of semantics, and we base our investigation on the three-step analytical process introduced in Lesson 6. Don't worry about the conditions in our example being non-disjoint; the analysis in **Step 1** will reconstitute the disjoint conditions.

Step 1. *Push the selection precondition into the selection statement.*

We determine the preconditions for the selection code segments by pushing the selection precondition into the statement. Pushing the precondition in this case, however, is not quite as simple as in the case of one-way selection. There is a ripple effect which must be accounted for as the precondition is pushed into each subsequent if-statement. We do this one step at a time. In this case the precondition is the postcondition of the call to GetBoundedLow. When we push this condition into the first (outer-most) if-statement we get the following. Notice that we have reinstated the indentation to emphasize the actual structure of the C^{++} if-statement:

```
GetBoundedLow(5, Customer);
// Assert: Customer >= 5

if (Customer <= 12)
    // Assert: 5 <= Customer <= 12
    Children = Children + 1;
else // Assert: Customer >= 5 AND Customer >= 13
    if (Customer <= 19)
        Teens = Teens + 1;
    else if (Customer <= 25)
        YoungAdults = YoungAdults + 1;
    else
        Adult = Adult + 1;
```

The condition on the else part simplifies to Customer >= 13 and becomes the precondition for the next if-statement. Pushing this precondition into its if-statement follows the same pattern and, with simplification, yields the following asserted code. Again notice that usual indentation has been applied to the inner if-statement:

```
GetBoundedLow(5, Customer);
// Assert: Customer >= 5

if (Customer <= 12)
    // Assert: 5 <= Customer <= 12
    Children = Children + 1;
else // Assert: Customer >= 13
    if (Customer <= 19)
        // Assert: 13 <= Customer <= 19
        Teens = Teens + 1;
    else // Assert: Customer >= 19
        if (Customer <= 25)
            YoungAdults = YoungAdults + 1;
        else
            Adult = Adult + 1;
```

Finally, we push the new precondition into the innermost if-statement. After simplification we get the following code segment:

```
GetBoundedLow(5, Customer);
// Assert: Customer >= 5

if (Customer <= 12)
    // Assert: 5 <= Customer <= 12
    Children = Children + 1;
else // Assert: Customer >= 13
    if (Customer <= 19)
        // Assert: 13 <= Customer <= 19
        Teens = Teens + 1;
    else // Assert: Customer >= 19
        if (Customer <= 25)
            // Assert: 20 <= Customer <= 25
            YoungAdults = YoungAdults + 1;
        else // Assert: Customer >= 26
            Adult = Adult + 1;
```

This completes the analytical process for finding preconditions for code segments. Now we need to put the code into a form appropriate for persuasive programming. First, we undo the indentation, whose only purpose was to highlight the nested one-way structure of the three-way selection. Second, the assertions which follow the first two elses should be seen as intermediate results on the way to the preconditions for the code segments. For this reason we eliminate these assertions. We are left with the code segment below in which each of the four code segments has a precondition:

```
GetBoundedLow(5, Customer);
// Assert: Customer >= 5

if (Customer <= 12)
    // Assert: 5 <= Customer <= 12
    Children = Children + 1;
else if (Customer <= 19)
    // Assert: 13 <= Customer <= 19
    Teens = Teens + 1;
else if (Customer <= 25)
    // Assert: 20 <= Customer <= 25
    YoungAdults = YoungAdults + 1;
else // Assert: Customer >= 26
    Adult = Adult + 1;
```

Oddly enough, in this exercise of finding the preconditions we have rediscovered the original disjoint selection conditions. Remember that we earlier simplified the conditions to gain a slimmed down and more efficient statement form.

The point to remember from this step is that pushing a precondition into an *n*-way selection takes separate steps for each condition, with the result of the previous push affecting the next push.

Step 2. *Determine code segment postconditions.*

The postconditions for each code segment are determined by appealing to assignment semantics. The following asserted code results:

```
GetBoundedLow(5, Customer);
// Assert: Customer >= 5

if (Customer <= 12)
    // Assert: 5 <= Customer <= 12
    Children = Children + 1;
    // Assert: 5 <= Customer <= 12 AND
    // Children == (pre)Children + 1
else if (Customer <= 19)
    // Assert: 13 <= Customer <= 19
    Teens = Teens + 1;
    // Assert: 13 <= Customer <= 19 AND
    // Teens == (pre)Teens + 1
else if (Customer <= 25)
    // Assert: 20 <= Customer <= 25
    YoungAdults = YoungAdults + 1;
    // Assert: 20 <= Customer <= 25 AND
```

```
      // YoungAdults == (pre)YoungAdults + 1
else // Assert: Customer >= 26
     Adult = Adult + 1;
     // Assert: Customer >= 26 AND
     // Adult == (pre)Adult + 1
```

Because the preconditions are disjoint and each postcondition is the conjunction of its precondition and another expression, the postconditions of these code segments are disjoint.

Step 3. *Determine the statement postcondition.*

Finally, we turn our attention to finding a postcondition for our three-way selection statement. We can proceed just as we did in determining the preconditions for the code segments – treat the three-way selection as a sequence of one-way selections with default. Now, if we follow this plan it is clear that we cannot determine a postcondition for the first one-way selection until we determine a postcondition for the first selection's else-part. A similar statement can be made for the second one-way selection. We must start at the inside with the third one-way selection and work our way out. The third one-way selection taken alone can be asserted as follows:

```
if (Customer <= 25)
     // Assert: 20 <= Customer <= 25
     YoungAdults = YoungAdults + 1;
else // Assert: Customer >= 26
     Adult = Adult + 1;
// Assert: (20 <= Customer <= 25 AND
//              YoungAdults == (pre)YoungAdults + 1)
//              OR
//          (Customer >= 26 AND
//              Adult == (pre)Adult + 1)
```

The code-segment postconditions have been suppressed as our persuasive programming guidelines indicate.

If we continue to determine the postcondition for the second one-way selection we begin with the following code segment. The indentation, which was removed earlier, has been restored to emphasize that the recently determined postcondition belongs to the third one-way selection:

```
if (Customer <= 19)
    // Assert: 13 <= Customer <= 19
    Teens = Teens + 1;
    // Assert: 13 <= Customer <= 19 AND
    // Teens == (pre)Teens + 1
else if (Customer <= 25)
        // Assert: 20 <= Customer <= 25
        YoungAdults = YoungAdults + 1;
     else // Assert: Customer >= 26
```

```
        Adult = Adult + 1;
  // Assert: (20 <= Customer <= 25 AND
  //             YoungAdults == (pre)YoungAdults + 1)
  //             OR
  //          (Customer >= 26 AND
  //             Adult == (pre)Adult + 1)
```

Now, following the rules for one-way selection postconditions, we determine the following postcondition for the second one-way selection:

```
if (Customer <= 19)
    // Assert: 13 <= Customer <= 19
    Teens = Teens + 1;
else if (Customer <= 25)
        // Assert: 20 <= Customer <= 25
        YoungAdults = YoungAdults + 1;
      else // Assert: Customer >= 26
        Adult = Adult + 1;
  // Assert: (13 <= Customer <= 19 AND
  //             Teens == (pre)Teens + 1)
  //             OR
  //          ( (20 <= Customer <= 25 AND
  //               YoungAdults == (pre)YoungAdults + 1)
  //               OR
  //            (Customer >= 26 AND
  //               Adult == (pre)Adult + 1) )
```

One important thing to notice here is that, since the OR operation is associative, we can drop the extra parentheses around the else-part's postcondition. Now, if we do some reformatting, we can see what has emerged – after all, what we have now is a postcondition for a two-way selection with default.

```
if (Customer <= 19)
    // Assert: 13 <= Customer <= 19
    Teens = Teens + 1;
else if (Customer <= 25)
    // Assert: 20 <= Customer <= 25
    YoungAdults = YoungAdults + 1;
else // Assert: Customer >= 26
    Adult = Adult + 1;
  // Assert: (13 <= Customer <= 19 AND
  //             Teens == (pre)Teens + 1)
  //             OR
  //          (20 <= Customer <= 25 AND
  //             YoungAdults == (pre)YoungAdults + 1)
  //             OR
  //          (Customer >= 26 AND
  //             Adult == (pre)Adult + 1)
```

This has worked out well. The postcondition for this two-way selection is just the disjunction of the postconditions for the three code segments. In fact, this is the general pattern – the postcondition for an n-way selection statement is just the disjunction of the postconditions for the code segments — so the postcondition for the original three-way selection statement should be as follows:

```
// Assert: Customer >= 5

if (Customer <= 12)
    // Assert: 5 <= Customer <= 12
    Children = Children + 1;
else if (Customer <= 19)
    // Assert: 13 <= Customer <= 19
    Teens = Teens + 1;
else if (Customer <= 25)
    // Assert: 20 <= Customer <= 25
    YoungAdults = YoungAdults + 1;
else // Assert: Customer >= 26
    Adult = Adult + 1;
// Assert: (5 <= Customer <= 12   AND
//              Children == (pre)Children + 1)
//                OR
//          (13 <= Customer <= 19 AND
//            Teens == (pre)Teens + 1)
//                OR
//          (20 <= Customer <= 25 AND
//            YoungAdults == (pre)YoungAdults + 1)
//                OR
//          (Customer >= 26 AND
//            Adult == (pre)Adult + 1)
```

This is, of course, what you would hope for the semantics of a generalization – that the pattern established for the original statement would be extended to the semantics for the generalized form.

11.3   Semantics of n-way Selection – A General Form

In order to arrive at a general representation for the semantics of the n-way selection statement, we must examine two points in a bit more detail and remind ourselves of a third.

Postconditions

First, remember that in **Step 2** of our analytical process we wrote each code segment postcondition as the conjunction of the segment precondition and another expression. While our analysis above is correct, it is important to remember that the precondition need not remain true in the post-state of the segment. A more general postcondition could be described as follows: if a segment has a precondition C, then its postcondition can be written as

```
(pre)C AND P
```

where P is an expression and `(pre)C` refers to the condition obtained from C by adding the prefix `(pre)` to each variable in C. Of course, if no variable appearing in C is modified in the segment, then `(pre)C` and C are the same, as is the case for each of the segments in the example above.

Selection Conditions and Preconditions

Second, at the end of the example above, it was pointed out that by following the push process we had rediscovered the original disjoint selection conditions. The obvious questions are: "Does this process always produce disjoint conditions?" and "Why does this process work?" Rather than give a completely general answer to these questions, we will look at a three-way selection statement where the conditions and segments are represented by identifiers. By following the push process with this general example, we will see how the disjoint conditions come about, thus answering both of the questions above. Here is the general form; we make no assumptions about whether the conditions C1, C2, and C3 are disjoint:

```
if (C1)
    S1;
else if (C2)
    S2;
else if (C3)
    S3;
else
    S4;
```

Let's follow the push process one step at a time and see what sort of preconditions emerge. Since there is no precondition for this general statement we can think of pushing the condition **true**.

```
if (C1)
    // Assert: C1
    S1;
else // Assert: NOT C1
    ...
```

The precondition for S1 and the precondition for what follows **else** are certainly disjoint. We will see in subsequent steps the condition (NOT C1) pushed into every precondition as a conjunct. This means that subsequent preconditions can be true only if C1 is false – i.e., C1, the first precondition, will be disjoint

from all subsequent preconditions. When (NOT C1) is pushed into the next
one-way selection we get the following additional assertions. Notice how (NOT
C1) appears as a conjunct in each one:

```
if (C1)
    // Assert: C1
    S1;
else // Assert: NOT C1
    if (C2)
        // Assert: (NOT C1) AND C2
        S2;
    else // Assert: (NOT C1) AND (NOT C2)
        ...
```

As predicted, the preconditions for S1 and S2 are disjoint. Notice that the
assertion following the last **else** is the conjunction of the negation of each of
the first two conditions. In other words, to get to this second **else** both of the
first two conditions must be false. Pushing the second **else**'s assertion into the
final one-way selection yields the following asserted code segment:

```
if (C1)
    // Assert: C1
    S1;
else // Assert: NOT C1
    if (C2)
        // Assert: (NOT C1) AND C2
        S2;
    else // Assert: (NOT C1) AND (NOT C2)
        if (C3)
            // Assert: (NOT C1) AND (NOT C2) AND C3
            S3;
        else // Assert: (NOT C1) AND (NOT C2) AND (NOT C3)
            S4;
```

If we look at the four statement preconditions,

```
C1
(NOT C1) AND C2
(NOT C1) AND (NOT C2) AND C3
(NOT C1) AND (NOT C2) AND (NOT C3)
```

we see two interesting things. Not only are these conditions disjoint, but given
any program state, one of the conditions is true. In this case we say the conditions *partition* the program state – or simply that the conditions are a partition.

In this demonstration we have made no assumption about whether the selection conditions are disjoint. If the selection conditions are not disjoint, the
process just demonstrated will determine a set of selection conditions which
are a partition. What if some of the conditions are disjoint but not all? A
convenient logical fact to know is that

if conditions A and B are disjoint then (NOT A) AND B reduces to B.

So if, in the general three-way selection above, it is known that the conditions C1 and C3 are disjoint, then the segment preconditions can be rewritten as follows:

```
C1
(NOT C1) AND C2
(NOT C2) AND C3
(NOT C1) AND (NOT C2) AND (NOT C3)
```

If all three conditions, C1, C2, C3, are known to be disjoint, then the preconditions can be rewritten as follows:

```
C1
C2
C3
(NOT C1) AND (NOT C2) AND (NOT C3)
```

The General Form

Before writing down a general form for the semantics of n-way selection, we should look back to the discussion of one-way semantics in Lesson 6. There we discovered that in order to accurately describe the semantics of one-way selection without default we still had to take into account the situation where the selection condition fails. We took advantage of the following equivalence:

```
// Assert: pre          // Assert: pre
if (C)                  if (C)
    S;                      S;
                        else
                            ;
```

In other words, in order to determine the semantics of one-way selection without default we had to convert to an equivalent one-way selection *with* default. So from a semantic point of view, all one-way selection statements have a default code segment. The same argument, not surprisingly, holds for the more general n-way selection statement: if there is no default, the state doesn't change, and that only happens when none of the selection conditions hold. So we can give the following general description for the semantics of the n-way selection statement. We make the following assumptions and observations:

- The conditions C1,...,Cn are disjoint.
- The conditions S1post,...,Snpost,S(n+1)post are the post-conditions resulting from appropriate preconditions on the corresponding code segments. In particular, it is assumed that the selection precondition, pre, was part of the code segment preconditions and, consequently, is represented in the postconditions listed.

- The default code segment S(n+1) might consist of only the do-nothing statement.

```
// Assert: pre
if (C1)
    S1;
else if (C2)
    S2;
    .

    .

    .
else if (Cn)
    Sn;
else
    S(n+1);
// Assert: ((pre)C1 AND S1post) OR
//         ((pre)C2 AND S2post) OR
//         ...
//         ((pre)Cn AND Snpost) OR
//         (NOT ((pre)C1 OR (pre)C2 OR
//                     ... OR (pre)Cn) AND
//            S(n+1)post)
```

11.4   Semantics of the switch Statement

The earlier indication that C^{++} has no n-way selection statement is not quite true. The switch statement is a special form of n-way selection where each condition must be satisfied by a single value of type int, char, or enum.[2] In a switch statement no conditions are specified – just the values are mentioned. In the following, the segment of code in the left column prints the age range for a given range designator; the code in the right column is an equivalent statement using our C^{++} four-way selection structure.

---

[2] enum is used to define what are called *enumerated types*. A common example is defining a type for color values as follows:

```
colors = enum{red, green, blue};
```

A variable of type colors can have one of three values: red, green, or blue.

```
typedef AgeCategory = {child, teenager, youngAdult, adult};
AgeCategory Age;
```

```
switch (Age) {                          if (Age == child)
  case child:                               cout << "5 - 12  years"
      cout << "5 - 12  years"                   << endl;
          << endl;                      else if (Age == teenager)
      break;                                cout << "13 - 19 years"
  case teenager:                              << endl;
      cout << "13 - 19 years"
          << endl;                      else if (Age == youngAdult)
      break;                                cout << "20 - 25 years"
  case youngAdult:                            << endl;
      cout << "20 - 25 years"           else if (Age == adult)
          << endl;                          cout << ">= 26 years"
      break;                                  << endl;
  case adult:
      cout << ">= 26 years"
          << endl;
      break;
```

With this simple equivalence, it is clear that the semantics of a `switch` statement will be the same as the semantics of the corresponding n-way selection statement. The following assertion is an appropriate postcondition for the statements above:

```
// Assert: (Age == child       AND
//              outstream == (pre)outstream + "5 - 12years\n")
//             OR
//          (Age == teenager    AND
//              outstream == (pre)outstream + "13 - 19 years\n")
//             OR
//          (Age == YoungAdult AND
//              outstream == (pre)outstream + "20 - 25 years\n")
//             OR
//          (Age == adult       AND
//              outstream == (pre)outstream + ">= 26 years\n")
```

11.5 An Alternative Logic for Selection Semantics

The semantics of n-way selection has been described in terms of the disjunction of postconditions for each code segment of the selection. The rationale behind this description is as follows. Since at most one of the code segments of the selection will be executed, we can count on at most one of the postconditions to be true – more postconditions can be true, but we can count on at most one being true. The disjunction of the postconditions expresses this condition.

There is an alternative way of expressing the semantics of n-way selection, one that is based on a logical operation we have not explicitly used to this point. This logical operation is called *implication*, and it corresponds to what we know as the if-then statement, i.e., one-way selection without default.

Logical Implication

Logical implication is a binary operation akin to logical conjunction and disjunction. If A and B are logical expressions then we write $A \longrightarrow B$ and read "if A then B" or "A implies B." In this expression we say that A is the *hypothesis* and B is the *conclusion*. In other words, the expression $A \longrightarrow B$ is true if whenever the hypothesis is true, then the conclusion is also true. "But what if the hypothesis is false?" you ask. In this case the logical implication is also true. So $A \longrightarrow B$ is true just in case A is false or both A and B are true, i.e., just in case $\neg A \vee (A \wedge B)$ is true. We can simplify this expression as follows:

$$
\begin{aligned}
A \longrightarrow B \quad &\equiv \quad \neg A \vee (A \wedge B) \\
&\equiv \quad (\neg A \vee A) \wedge (\neg A \vee B) \\
&\equiv \quad (\neg A \vee B)
\end{aligned}
$$

This final expression in this simplification is the standard definition for logical implication.

Alternative Description for n-way Semantics

How, then, does logical implication provide an alternative for describing the semantics of n-way selection? It is really quite straightforward. Let's assume that we have a selection statement with n disjoint conditions as follows:

```
// Assert: Spre
if (C1)
    S1;
    // Assert: S1post
else if (C2)
    S2;
    // Assert: S2post
else .

      .

      .
else if (Cn)
    Sn;
    // Assert: Snpost
else
    S(n+1);
    // Assert: S(n+1)post
```

Since the conditions are disjoint, only one can be true in a given state. For the condition which is true, the corresponding postcondition will also be true; for the conditions, all of which must be false, it doesn't matter how the corresponding postcondition evaluates. What this says is that for each condition Ci, the implication "Ci $\longrightarrow$ Sipost" will be true. Additionally, if none of the conditions are true, then, since there is no default, the selection's precondition will be true. This means that the following can be adopted as the postcondition (i.e., semantics) for the selection statement:

```
( (pre)C1 --> S1post ) AND
( (pre)C2 --> S2post ) AND
   .
   .
   .
( (pre)Cn --> Snpost ) AND
( NOT (C1 OR C2 OR ... OR Cn) --> S(n+1)post )
```

It is important to recognize that the argument above relies on the assumption that the conditions are disjoint. If it happened that two conditions were true in the same state, the code segment for the first condition encountered would be executed, but only its postcondition could be guaranteed to be true – for the other condition we would have a true hypothesis (the condition), but the chance that the postcondition would be false.

Assuming the conditions are disjoint, the postcondition given above will be true after the selection is executed. The case described above is for an *n*-way selection without default; if the selection is specified *with* a default, then the postcondition would change only in the final component, with Spre being replaced by the postcondition for the default code segment.

Are the Semantic Representations the Same?

You may wonder if the two semantic representations are, in fact, equivalent – we certainly imply that they are. We need to argue that the two forms will be always be true for the same states. If we assume that one form is true and show that the other must be true and vice versa, then we have shown the forms are equivalent. The two forms we want to prove to be equivalent are as follows:

Form1 – (C1 AND P1) OR ... OR (Cn AND Pn)
Form2 – (C1 ==> P1) AND ... AND (Cn ==> Pn).

We make the following assumptions about the conditions that appear in these two forms:

1. The conditions C1,...,Cn form a partition for the possible program states.

2. For each condition P1,...,Pn we assume that if Ci is true then Pi is also true. This is justified because each condition Pi represents a postcondition which is deduced from the condition Ci as well as other conditions.

Assume Form1 is true:

> If **Form1** is true, then one of the expressions in the disjunction must be true – assume it is `Ci AND Pi`. If this conjunction is true then both `Ci` and `Pi` are true. Since both `Ci` and `Pi` are true, `Ci ==> Pi` is also true by the definition of `==>`. Also, since `Ci` is true and the conditions `C1,...,Cn` form a partition, all the other implications in **Form2** are also true because their hypotheses are all false. This means that when **Form1** is true, so is **Form2**.

Assume Form2 is true:

> If **Form2** is true then all of the expressions in the conjunction must be true. Because the conditions `C1,...,Cn` form a partition of the possible program states, one of these hypotheses must be true and all the others must be false. If the hypothesis `Ci` is the true one, then since `Ci ==> Pi` is true, the condition `Pi` must also be true. This means that `Ci AND Pi` is true and, because **Form1** is a disjunction, **Form1** must be true.

These two arguments together show that the two forms for n-way semantics are equivalent. The two examples that follow show selection statements asserted with postconditions in both forms:

Example 24 – Asserting a selection statement (I)
▼

```
      // Assert: X, Y have values

      if (X < Y)
           Y = Y - X;
      else // Assert: Y <= X
           Y = X - Y;
      // Assert: [Original Form]
      //         (Y >= 0) AND
      //         ( (X < (pre)Y AND Y == (pre)Y - X) OR
      //             ((pre)Y <= X AND Y == X - (pre)Y) )
      // Assert: [Implication Form]
      //         (Y >= 0) AND
      //         ( (X < (pre)Y  --> Y == (pre)Y - X) AND
      //             ((pre)Y <= X --> Y == X - (pre)Y) )
```

▲

Example 25 – **Asserting a selection statement (II)**
▼

```
        // Assert: Customer >= 5

        if (Customer <= 12)
            // Assert: 5 <= Customer <= 12
            Children = Children + 1;
        else if (Customer <= 19)
            // Assert: 13 <= Customer <= 19
            Teens = Teens + 1;
        else if (Customer <= 25)
            // Assert: 20 <= Customer <= 25
            YoungAdults = YoungAdults + 1;
        else // Assert: Customer >= 26
            Adult = Adult + 1;
        // Assert: [Original Form]
        //          (5 <= Customer <= 12  AND
        //           Children == (pre)Children + 1)
        //                 OR
        //          (13 <= Customer <= 19 AND
        //           Teens == (pre)Teens + 1)
        //                 OR
        //          (20 <= Customer <= 25 AND
        //           YoungAdults == (pre)YoungAdults + 1)
        //                 OR
        //          (Customer >= 26        AND
        //           Adult == (pre)Adult + 1)
        // Assert: [Implication Form]
        //          (5 <= Customer <= 12  -->
        //                Children == (pre)Children + 1)
        //             AND
        //          (13 <= Customer <= 19 -->
        //                Teens == (pre)Teens + 1)
        //             AND
        //          (20 <= Customer <= 25 -->
        //                YoungAdults == (pre)YoungAdults + 1)
        //             AND
        //          (Customer >= 26        -->
        //                Adult == (pre)Adult + 1)
```

▲

Lesson 12

More on Repetition

In Lesson 7 we investigated the semantics of the `while` loop. In the process we discovered that it is important to understand the cumulative effect of repeatedly executing the loop body. We looked at one example, an input validation loop, in which the processing on one pass had no effect on the processing of subsequent passes. In fact, when the validation loop terminates it is impossible to know, based on the loop's resulting value, whether or not the loop body was ever executed (at least not without looking at the program's output).

Most loops, however, don't have this nice characteristic of non-accumulation, and understanding their semantics is more difficult. We looked at a couple of these accumulation loops in Lesson 7, one for which accumulation happened on every pass (finding the sum of the first X positive integers) and another where accumulation occurred only if a certain condition was true (finding the largest value in a list). One technique we used to understand what was happening in these loops was to unwind the loop, i.e., to look at the loop as a code segment made up of a sequence of copies of the loop body. By looking at the loop in this "stretched out" way it was a bit easier to determine an assertion which described the functioning of the loop.

In this lesson we will look again at the problem of asserting a loop with the goal to identify a better strategy – a strategy which will bring increased clarity to loop semantics. In the process we will introduce two new ideas: the *loop variant*, which is related to loop termination, and the *loop invariant*, a condition which is meant to represent the cumulative effect of a loop's execution. We begin with the often heard loop termination question.

12.1 But Will It Ever End? (The Loop Variant)

The loop invariant, which we will investigate shortly, is a condition which is true before and after each execution of a loop's body – as we indicated above, its purpose is to characterize the cumulative effect of executing a loop. What the loop invariant may not indicate, however, is whether a loop will ever terminate.

Generating an infinite loop seems to be one of the more common activities of programming students. In this section we will look at a way of guarding against this common, and often difficult to find, error – our tool will be the *loop variant*.

If the loop *invariant* is a condition which is true before and after each pass through the loop body, then the loop *variant* must be something which is *not* the same. In fact, the loop variant is an expression which reflects the amount of data that has not yet been processed. Let's revisit the "sum of positive integers" algorithm which we studied in Lesson 7 (page 95):

```
Count = 0;
Sum   = 0;
while (Count < X) {
       Count = Count + 1;
       Sum = Sum + Count;
}
```

It is pretty clear from this loop that the body will be executed X times. The variable Count in a sense keeps track of how many times the loop has been executed so far, so the number of passes remaining (when the loop starts) is always given by the expression X - Count; this expression is the loop variant. Notice that this variant will be zero when Count equals X.

What is important about this loop variant? On every pass through the loop the value of Count increases and, since the value of X remains the same, the value of the loop variant decreases; when it gets to 0 the loop terminates. We want to represent the loop variant somehow in the structure of the loop as a reminder that we must be sure to decrease it on each pass. We assert the loop as follows:

```
Count = 0;
Sum   = 0;
while // Variant: X - Count >= 0
       (Count < X) {
       Count = Count + 1; // Assert: variant decreases here
       Sum = Sum + Count;
}
// Assert: Count == X
```

Before considering the odd location of the Variant comment, what happened to the loop variant? It seems to have been pulled into a condition. Though the loop variant is our focus, we do our reasoning about semantics through assertions, i.e., conditions. We will call the condition in the Variant comment the *loop variant condition* – it will usually say that the loop variant is greater than or equal to zero.

Now back to the odd location of the Variant. This location is used because it emphasizes that the variant is relevant before the loop starts and after each execution of the loop body, i.e., always just before the loop condition is checked. The variant could be placed just before the loop and then at the end of the loop body, but that would create clutter. Another reason is by putting the variant between the `while` and the loop condition, the variant is made to appear as a natural part of the loop syntax.

Identifying the loop variant is an important step in understanding a loop, but of equal importance is to identify in the loop body what statement causes the loop variant to decrease. The combination of the identification of the loop variant and location in the code where the variant decreases gives us assurance that the loop will terminate.

In the example above, it was possible to represent the number of passes remaining in terms of variables in the environment. When the loop is driven by input, however, this may not be the case.

Example 26 – Determine the highest input value
▼

We will take another look at the algorithm for finding the largest input value – this was investigated in Lesson 9.1.

```
Hi = 0;

GetNatural (Val);
while (Val > 0) {
      if (Val > Hi)
         Hi = Val;

      GetNatural (Val);
}
```

Determining how many passes through the loop remain is difficult because the data is entered interactively. There's no way for the programmer to know or find out what it will be. Remember that in the last example we had a record of how many passes would take place – it was just the value of X. We have no such variable here. We need a strategy. Here it is:

1. We can assume that there will be a finite number of input values and that the last one will be zero (or less). Though it is possible for a user to sit there entering a potentially infinite list of values, it is not the intended use of the algorithm, so we ignore the infinite case and concentrate on the finite one.

2. We will assert a sequence of values on the input stream and use "Len" to denote the number of values remaining in the stream.

```
// Assert: in stream has v1,...,vn,0
//         For I = 1,...,n: vI > 0
//         Len denotes number of input values remaining
//         Len == n+1
```

Notice that each time the algorithm reads a value from the input stream the value of Len decreases by one. Len is the loop variant.

3. Use the condition Len >= 0 as the loop variant assertion.

Following this analysis we have the following asserted loop:

```
Hi = 0;

// Assert: in stream has v1,...,vn,0
//         For I = 1,...,n: vI > 0
//         Len denotes number of input values remaining
//         Len == n+1
GetNatural (Val); // Assert: Len decreases by 1
while // Variant: Len >= 0
      (Val > 0) {
      if (Val > Hi)
         Hi = Val;

      GetNatural (Val); // Assert: Len decreases by 1
}
// Assert: Len == 0
```

▲

The watchful reader may be itching to ask the following question:

> *The loop invariant is a condition which is true before and after each pass through the loop body. Each variant condition we have seen seems to have this property! Why aren't these loop variants combined into the loop invariant?*

Good question. The answer is that it is useful to separate the termination condition from the loop invariant. In fact, we will see below that we treat the loop invariant in very much the same way we do the variant condition above.

12.2   Revisiting the Generic Loop

The first thing we will do is look at the general case of a while loop and see what we can conclude about appropriate assertions. We can put assertions in four obvious places (we're leaving out the variant for now).

```
Initial;
// Assert: looppre  -- loop precondition
while (Cond)

        // Assert: bodypre  -- body precondition
        Body;
        // Assert: bodypost -- body postcondition

// Assert: looppost -- loop postcondition
```

Before trying to draw any conclusions about the characteristics of these assertions, we can make some general observations.

1. The condition `looppre` will be true on entering the loop, but may not be true for other passes through the loop. This means that we can't just push `looppre` into the loop.

2. At the point of the body precondition, the loop condition `Cond` is true. (This means that `Cond` could be part of `bodypre`.)

3. At the point of the body postcondition the loop condition *may* be false, and if it is the loop is about to terminate. (This means that `Cond` *cannot* be part of `bodypost`.)

4. At the point of the loop postcondition `Cond` must be false. But what else can we say? We would like to say that the `bodypost` must be true, but the only way this can be the case is if the loop body is actually executed. If the loop body is not executed this means that the loop condition was false on the first entry. But in this case the loop precondition will still be true. So the loop postcondition should be something like the following:

```
// Assert: (NOT Cond) AND (looppre OR bodypost)
```

Let's think more carefully about the body pre- and postconditions. Since `Cond` cannot be part of `bodypost` let's assume for a minute that it is also not part of `bodypre`. In this case, if `Cond` is true then `bodypre` was true at the bottom of the loop body as well. It would seem that `bodypre` and `bodypost` might be closely related – in fact, they might be the same. If we can find a condition, call it `bodyboth`, which can act as the body pre- and postconditions, then we can rewrite our standard loop as follows:

```
Initial;
// Assert: looppre
while (Cond)

        // Assert: bodyboth AND Cond
        Body;
        // Assert: bodyboth

// Assert: (NOT Cond) AND (looppre OR bodyboth)
```

This is looking a lot simpler than what we had originally. There are just three Boolean expressions in which we are interested: Cond, which is given as part of the code, looppre, which is determined from the initialization, and bodyboth, which, since it is always true before and after the loop, would seem to be the *loop invariant* referred to earlier.

12.3   The Loop Invariant

The definition given earlier indicated that the loop invariant is a condition which is true before and after each execution of the loop's body. This definition needs to be a bit more precise. In the previous section we argued that the conditions bodypre and bodypost should be thought of as the same. The only problem is that bodypre will be true *after* the loop condition is evaluated and bodypost will be true *before* the loop condition is evaluated. We can't have it both ways. Rather, we will choose the bodypost to be our bodyboth and we will assume it is true before the loop condition is evaluated. So our definition of loop invariant must be altered as follows:

> A *loop invariant* is a condition which is true each time before the loop condition is evaluated.

In this section we will look at several examples – some straightforward, others more complex – to get a better feel for what makes a good loop invariant. As we will see, for a particular loop there may be several different possibilities for loop invariant – our goal is to find the one that tells us the most. Another issue we will address is where should we place the loop invariant.

We begin with another visit to our favorite example – sum the first X positive integers. We will look at three different loop invariants for this example and see which one seems to best reflect the actions of the loop. We will also include the loop variant condition we determined in Example 26.

Loop Invariant – A First Attempt

We are looking for a loop invariant for the loop which sums the positive integers from 1 up through the value of X. Our first attempt at a loop invariant follows:

```
// Assert: X > 0
Count = 0; Sum = 0;
// Assert: X > 0 AND Count == 0 AND Sum == 0
while // Variant: X - Count >= 0
      (Count < X) {
      // Assert: Sum has a value AND Count < X
      Count = Count + 1;
      Sum = Sum + Count;
      // Assert: Sum has a value
}
// Assert: Count == X AND Sum has a value
```

The loop invariant "`Sum has a value`" is true before and after each execution of the loop body – this is what we want!

But how do we like this attempt at a loop invariant? It does satisfy our definition, but it doesn't seem to tell us much – it's not very interesting. The problem is that it doesn't put any restriction on what the value of `Sum` could be. Before going on to the next attempt, what about the location of the invariant? It seems silly to put it in the loop twice. What if we put it with the loop variant? This makes sense because it emphasizes the fact that the invariant is true before the loop starts, before and after the loop body executes, and at the point where the loop condition fails. We write the loop as follows:

```
// Assert: X > 0

Count = 0;
Sum   = 0;
// Assert: X > 0 AND Count == 0 AND Sum == 0
while // Variant:   X - Count >= 0
      // Invariant: Sum has a value
      (Count < X) {
      Count = Count + 1;
      Sum = Sum + Count;
}
// Assert: Count == X AND
//         Sum has a value
```

Now we return to our search for a good loop invariant. We need an invariant that puts limits on the value of `Sum`. One thing we know is that `Sum` starts out with value zero and then increases, because we are always adding a positive value to it. This means that on every pass through the loop the value of `Sum` must be positive or zero. This implies the following loop invariant:

```
// Invariant: Sum >= 0
```

Is this any good? Well, it is better since it is a stronger condition. But we still don't get any insight for the value that `Sum` really has.

Loop Invariant – A Second Attempt

Our previous attempts at loop invariants didn't say much about the functioning of the loop because the condition is satisfied by too many values. In fact, the conditions we have seen so far are invariants for lots of different loops. We would like an invariant that works for this loop but not for any other loops. We need more restriction – this means more careful analysis. If we return to page 95 and look at the unwinding of our loop we can see that another fact about `Sum` which is always true is `Sum >= Count`. Now this is more restrictive.

```
// Assert: X > 0

Count = 0;
Sum   = 0;
// Assert: X > 0 AND Count == 0 AND Sum == 0
while // Variant:    X - Count >= 0
      // Invariant: Sum >= Count
      (Count < X) {
      Count = Count + 1;
      Sum = Sum + Count;
}
// Assert: Count == X AND
//         Sum >= X
```

But we can restrict things even more. We know, for example, that the following condition also serves as an invariant:

```
// Invariant: Count <= Sum <= Count*Count
```

Examples

The previous two subsections show that there is a range of possible invariants for a particular loop. In fact, we can add an even simpler one to our list: "**true**" is an invariant for every loop. These invariants are inadequate because they are too weak – they do not come close enough to characterizing the result of executing the loop, which should be a specific value for Sum. Fortunately, back in Lesson 7.2 we did this kind of careful analysis and came up with a better invariant.

```
Sum == 1 + ...   + Count
```

If we put this condition together with the other invariants we have examined we notice an interesting thing.

```
Sum == 1 + ...   + Count

Count <= Sum <= Count*Count

Sum >= Count

Sum has a value

true
```

Moving down the list we go from stronger to weaker conditions. When we talk about *the* loop invariant of a loop we will always mean the strongest loop invariant. Here are a few more examples of loops and possible invariants:

Example 27 – Division algorithm

▼

```
// Assert: Num >= 0 AND Div > 0
Q = 0;
R = Num;

// Assert: Q == 0 AND R == Num
while // Variant:   R - Div >= 0
      // Invariant: ???
      (R >= Div) {
      R = R - Div; // loop variant decreases
      Q = Q + 1;
}
// Assert: 0 <= R < Div
```

The loop variant need not give the exact number of passes through the loop, it just has to register the progress that is being made toward termination. In this case we know that if the loop condition fails, then the loop variant will go negative.

But what about a loop invariant? The loop works by decomposing the value in Num into a multiple of Div plus a remainder R; on each pass Div is subtracted from R, and Q is incremented to account for the subtraction. The following conditions both work, but the second is the stronger and clearly says more about the actual values of the variables:

```
Q and R have values
Num == Q*Div + R
```

But it is still not the loop invariant. What is missing? If the loop is entered then we know that R >= Div is true. This means that after R is decremented by Div, R cannot be less than zero. Since R starts out with value Num which is non-negative, then R >= 0 is always true. This should be added to the second condition above to get the loop invariant.

Here is the final form of the loop. Notice that the loop's postcondition follows from the fact that the loop invariant is true after the loop and the loop condition is false:

```
// Assert: Num >= 0 AND Div > 0
Q = 0;
R = Num;

// Assert: Q == 0 AND R == Num
while // Variant:   R - Div >= 0
      // Invariant: Num == Q*Div + R AND R >= 0
```

```
                (R >= Div) {
                R = R - Div; // loop variant decreases
                Q = Q + 1;
        }
        // Assert: Num == Q*Div + R AND
        //              0 <= R < Div
```

The postcondition here has been simplified from the following condition, which you might have expected to see.

```
        // Assert: Num == Q*Div + R AND R >= 0 AND R < Div
```

▲

Example 28 – Sequential search algorithm
▼

The following loop is at the heart of the sequential search algorithm. According to the code segment's precondition we have access to a list of values with zero or more elements and a target value for which we will search the list.

```
// Assert: NItems >= 0 AND
//         T has a value AND
//         For I = 0,...,(NItems-1): List[I] has a value
Found = false;
I     = 0;
while // Variant: NItems - I >= 0
      (!Found && (I < NItems)) {
      if (T == List[I])
        Found = true;
      else
        I = I + 1; // Assert: invariant decreases here
}
// Assert: Found OR I == NItems
```

(A comment on the loop variant: The purpose of the variant is to provide evidence that the loop will eventually terminate. In this example the invariant is decreased only if the search is to continue; if it is not to continue then Found is set and the loop terminates anyway. So NItems - I does give an *upper bound* to the number of passes through the loop. We know that if the target is not found then the variant will become zero.)

Remember that the loop invariant should be true before *and* after the loop body executes. So let's concentrate on *after* first. If we recall what we learned about the semantics of the one-way selection statement, then the loop body can be asserted as follows:

```
// Assert: !Found AND (I < NItems)

if (T == List[I])
      Found = true;
else I = I + 1;

// Assert: ( Found  AND  T == List[(pre)I] AND
//              (pre)I < NItems)
//                    OR
//          ( !Found AND  T != List[(pre)I] AND
//              (pre)I < NItems)
```

This postcondition can be simplified a bit since the value (pre)I can be determined in each of the components. If Found is true, then the value of I doesn't change, so (pre)I can be replaced by I. When Found is false, on the other hand, we know that I has been increased at the point of the assertion. So in the second component, the (pre)I can be replace by I-1. We arrive at the following loop body postcondition:

```
( Found  AND  T == List[I]   AND I <  NItems) OR
( !Found AND  T != List[I-1] AND I <= NItems)
```

Now we are in a position to track down a loop invariant. This time we won't announce it – we will figure it out using the technique of loop unwinding introduced in Lesson 7. Here is an unwinding of four passes, where we find the target on the fourth pass. What we want to track down is any cumulative effect of executing the loop. You will notice that we write down the above postcondition after each loop body execution, but then simplify that postcondition for inclusion in the precondition of the next pass. The bit that is simplified each time is labelled with the "<<<---".

```
Found = false;
I = 0;

// Assert: !Found AND I < NItems AND
//         I == 0
if (T == List[I])
     Found = true;
else I = I + 1;
// Assert: !Found AND I == 1 AND
//         ( Found  AND  T == List[0] AND
//           0 <  NItems)
//              OR
//         ( !Found AND  T != List[0] AND
```

```
//           1 <= NItems)                      <<<---


// Assert: !Found AND I < NItems AND
//          T != List[0] AND I == 1
if (T == List[I])
     Found = true;
else I = I + 1;
// Assert: T != List[0] AND !Found AND I == 1 AND
//          ( Found  AND  T == List[1] AND
//             1 <  NItems)
//               OR
//          ( !Found AND  T != List[1] AND
//            2 <= NItems)                     <<<---


// Assert: !Found AND I < NItems AND
//          T != List[0] AND T != List[1] AND
//          I == 2
if (T == List[I])
     Found = true;
else I = I + 1;
// Assert: T != List[0] AND T != List[1] AND
//         !Found AND I == 2 AND
//          ( Found  AND  T == List[2] AND
//            2 <  NItems)
//                OR
//          ( !Found AND  T != List[2] AND
//            3 <= NItems)                     <<<---


// Assert: !Found AND I < NItems AND
//          T != List[0] AND T != List[1] AND
//          T != List[2] AND I == 3
if (T == List[I])
     Found = true;
else I = I + 1;
// Assert: T != List[0] AND T != List[1] AND
//          T != List[2] AND I == 3
//          ( Found  AND  T == List[3] AND
//            3 <  NItems)
//                OR                           <<<---
//          ( !Found AND  T != List[3] AND
//            3 <= NItems)


// Assert: Found AND I < NItems AND I ==3 AND
//          T != List[0] AND T != List[1] AND
//          T != List[2] AND T == List[3]
```

In each postcondition in this unwinding, we see the accumulation of data representing the continuing failure to find the value of T in the array. This accumulation is missing from the body postcondition. The appropriate loop invariant, then, should be a combination of the body postcondition and this accumulation factor. In this invariant notice that it is true regardless of whether the pass causes I to be incremented.

```
For J = 0,...,I-1:T != List[J] AND
( ( Found  AND  T == List[I]   AND I <  NItems) OR
  ( !Found AND  T != List[I-1] AND I <= NItems) )
```

We know that this condition is true after every pass through the loop, but what about before the first pass? If we write the invariant for the initial state of the loop we will see that it is true, though it may look a bit odd.

```
For J = 0,...,-1:T != List[J] AND
( ( Found  AND  T == List[0]   AND I <  NItems) OR
  ( !Found AND  T != List[-1] AND I <= NItems) )
```

The two problem spots are obviously the occurrences of -1. A For expression is really an abbreviation for a conjunction, in this case a conjunction of no components – something like summing a set of values where the set is empty. In logic this "empty" conjunction is taken as true. The second occurrence of -1 is also strange but manageable. One's first reaction is that -1 is not possible as an array index since -1 indexes nothing in the array. But since our target T does have a value, we should clearly accept the fact that T is not equal to List[-1]. So before the first pass of the loop, our proposed invariant is true.

That's a lot of work, but in the end we feel that we really understand why the algorithm works. This, of course, is the whole idea of the persuasive programming style. After the above analysis we can write the following almost-complete code segment:

```
// Assert: NItems >= 0 AND
//         T has a value AND
//         For J = 0,...,(NItems-1): List[J] has a value
Found = false;
I     = 0;
while // Variant: NItems - I >= 0
      // Invariant: For J = 0,...,I-1:T != List[J] AND
      //                ( (Found  AND  T == List[I]   AND
      //                    I <  NItems)
      //                OR
      //                       OR
```

```
//                  (!Found AND  T != List[I-1]
//                      AND I <= NItems) )
    (!Found && (I < NItems)) {
    if (T == List[I])
          Found = true;
    else I = I + 1;
}
// Assert: (Found OR I == NItems) AND
//         (For J = 0,...,I-1:T != List[J]) AND
//         ( (Found  AND  T == List[I]     AND
//             I <  NItems)
//                 OR
//           (!Found AND  T != List[I-1] AND
//             I == NItems) )
```

The final postcondition can be simplified based on what we know about the values of Found and I. If we know that Found is true, then the clause on the third line of the assertion must be false. On the other hand, if Found is false (the only alternative to true!), then the clause on the second line of the postcondition is false. So the postcondition can be simplified to the following:

```
// Assert: For J = 0,...,I-1: T != List[J] AND
//         ( Found AND T == List[I] AND I <  NItems)
//              OR
//         (!Found AND I == NItems)
```

One important final comment on this example. We have seen two solutions to asserting the sequential search algorithm. The way to compare the two approaches is to say that the second says more about what the algorithm actually does, just as was the case in the first example of this section. For example, if the algorithm terminates without finding the target, the postcondition from the first approach only tells us that the last element of the list isn't the target. The second approach tells us that the target doesn't appear anywhere in the list. The first one isn't *incorrect*, it is just *incomplete*, and that is what separates good from not-so-good loop invariants.

▲

12.4   Nesting Repetitions

Here is a repetition statement which manipulates the values in an array of integers. The repetition is the "bubble up" of the dreaded bubble sort algorithm. Remember that the basic idea in bubbling up is to pass through the array comparing neighboring values – if the values are out of order, then swap them. You can see our assumptions for the algorithm in the code segment's precondition:

```
// Assert: NItems >= 0 AND
//          For I = 0,..,(NItems-1): A[I] has a value

I = 0;
while // Variant: NItems - I >= 1
   (I < NItems - 1) {
   if (A[I] > A[I+1]) swap(A[I], A[I+1]);
   I = I + 1; // Assert: variant (NItems - I)
              //              decreases here
}
// Assert: I == NItems - 1
```

A little thought will reveal that in one pass through the repetition the largest value in the array will be moved to the top position in the array – i.e., at position NItems-1. Here is the repetition properly asserted, complete with a loop invariant:

```
// Assert: NItems >= 0 AND
//          For I = 0,..,(NItems-1): A[I] has a value

I = 0;
while // Variant: NItems - I >= 1
      // Invariant: For J = 0,...,(I-1): A[I] > A[J]
      (I < NItems - 1) {
   if (A[I] > A[I+1]) swap(A[I], A[I+1]);
   I = I + 1; // Assert: variant (NItems - I)
              //              decreases here
}
// Assert: I == NItems - 1 AND
//          For J = 0,...,(NItems-2): A[NItems-1] > A[J]
```

Is it the best we can do? Notice that this condition says something about the relationship between the last element (at I) and every value earlier in the array, but it says nothing about the relative positions of the values before position I. Are they the same relative to their positions before the loop? Are they in some predictable order? Investigating a few examples shows that it is at least not easy to tell whether this is the best loop invariant we can come up with.

But there is another consideration. How is this bubble up algorithm to be used? It is used as part of the bubble sort algorithm, in which the bubble up part is applied to the first NItems values in the array, then to the first NItems-1 values, etc. It is clear that for the purposes of the bubble sort algorithm, the loop invariant we have identified guarantees the required property of the array. So, in specific instances, it is not necessary to guarantee that the loop invariant is the best possible – being guided by the context in which the loop is used can help determine an appropriate loop invariant.

To finish up this example, we will look at a complete bubble sort algorithm to see what happens when repetitions are nested. Here is an unasserted implementation of bubble sort:

```
// Assert: NItems >= 0 AND
//          For I = 0,..,(NItems-1): A[I] has a value

K = NItems;
while (K > 0) {
    I = 0;
    while (I < K - 1) {
        if (A[I] > A[I+1]) swap(A[I], A[I+1]);
        I = I + 1;
    }
    K = K - 1;
}
```

Just to refresh our memories, the bubble sort algorithm works as follows. It makes NItems-1 passes sequentially through the array, swapping adjacent array elements if they are found to be out of order (smaller to larger).

We discovered in analyzing the inner repetition that after one pass the largest element has reached its final position, at the highest indexed position. This repetition has been adapted to the bubble sort algorithm by changing the top limit of the array traversal. This takes advantage of the fact that, since the largest element makes its way to the top of the array, there is no need to go all the way to the end on the subsequent pass. We can easily adapt our earlier comments to this new inner loop.

```
// Assert: NItems >= 0 AND
//          For I = 0,..,(NItems-1): A[I] has a value

K = NItems-1;
while (K > 0) {
    I = 0;
    while // Variant: K - I >= 0
         // Invariant: For J = 0,...,(I-1): A[I] > A[J]
       (I < K) {
       if (A[I] > A[I+1]) swap(A[I], A[I+1]);
       I = I + 1; // Assert: variant (K-I)
                  //               decreases here
    }
    // Assert: I == K AND
    //          For J = 0,...,(K-1): A[K] > A[J]
    K = K - 1;
}
```

In thinking about the results of the inner repetition, we see clearly that the part of the loop from position K to the end is in sorted order. Each pass puts the largest value at position K and then decreases K, so the next pass puts the next smallest value at the new position K. We can summarize this in the following asserted statement:

```
// Assert: NItems >= 0 AND
//         For I = 0,..,(NItems-1): A[I] has a value

K = NItems-1;
while // Variant: K > 0
      // Invariant: For J = K+1,...,NItems-2:
      //                 A[J] <= A[J+1]
      (K > 0) {
      // bubble up goes here
      K = K - 1;   // Assert: variant (K)
                   //            decreases here
}
// Assert: For J = 1,...,NItems-2: A[J] <= A[J+1]
```

But this isn't quite right. The final assertion should read "J = 0", but it doesn't follow from the invariant of the outer repetition. What's wrong? We have taken one property from the inner repetition, but have left another behind. Our outer invariant says that the "end" of the array is always sorted, with "end" being defined by the value of K. But the inner loop also tells us that the values in the "beginning" of the array are all less than or equal to those at the end. This is the missing element in the outer invariant. Notice how this problem is resolved in both the outer invariant and the final assertion in the following complete asserted implementation:

```
// Assert: NItems >= 0 AND
//         For I = 0,..,(NItems-1): A[I] has a value
K = NItems-1;
while // Variant: K > 0
      // Invariant: For J = K+1,...,NItems-2:
      //                 A[J] <= A[J+1]
      //             AND
      //         For J = 0,...,K: A[K+1] >= A[J]
      (K > 0) {
      I = 0;
      while // Variant: K - I >= 0
            // Invariant: For J = 0,...,(I-1):
            //                 A[I] >= A[J]
            (I < K) {
            if (A[I] > A[I+1]) swap(A[I], A[I+1]);
            I = I + 1; // Assert: variant (K-I)
                       //            decreases here
      }
      // Assert: I == K AND
      //         For J = 0,...,(K-1): A[K] >= A[J]
      K = K - 1;   // Assert: variant (K) decreases here
}
// Assert: For J = 0,...,NItems-2: A[J] <= A[J+1]
```

12.5   Advanced – Deriving a Loop

In this section we will look at a more advanced technique for dealing with loops. What we will do is look at a requirement for a loop, in the form of pre- and postconditions, and then derive (working backwards) the three loop components so that they produce the specified postcondition.[1]

The problem is to determine whether a given positive integer is a prime number. Here are the pre- and postconditions that describe this problem:

```
// Assert: N > 0

Statement

// Assert: ( Answer == false AND
//               N is not prime ) OR
//             ( Answer == true  AND
//               N is prime )
```

This is clear enough, but how do we do anything with these simple conditions? They don't seem to give much to work with. The key, in fact, is right there in the postcondition – the term **prime** needs to be replaced by an expression which is true just when N is prime, i.e., a condition which defines primeness. By definition, a positive integer N is prime if it is greater than one and divisible only by itself and one – by "divisible" we mean integer division with no remainder. The following condition is a straightforward translation of this definition:

```
N > 1 AND
For I = 2,...,N-1: N % I != 0
```

Now, the postcondition above refers not just to **prime** but also to **not prime**. Using the logical rules for negating a conjunction and negating a universal (see Appendix A) we see that **not prime** can be replaced by the following expression:

```
N = 1 OR
There is I: 2 <= I < N AND N % I == 0
```

With these new expressions substituted into the postcondition, our code segment for determining primeness has the following structure:

```
// Assert: N > 0

Statement

// Assert: ( Answer == false AND
```

---

[1]Note: This section is not here because you are expected to immediately be able to carry out a similar analysis. The idea is to illustrate what is possible in applying assertion-based semantics. You should read through the example, follow the steps carefully, and then in future projects, watch for similar patterns. Your intuition will improve in the process.

```
//                ( N == 1           OR
//                   There is I: 2 <= I < N AND N % I == 0 ) ) OR
//                ( Answer == true   AND
//                  N > 1            AND
//                  For I = 2,...,N-1: N % I != 0 )
```

And the big question is what should `Statement` be replaced by so that when the precondition is true the postcondition is guaranteed to be true? We know that `Statement` will not be replaced by something as simple as a sequence of assignment statements, so `Statement` will be a selection or repetition or a combination of the two. The advantage we gain from the previous lessons is that we know the form of postconditions for these two types of statements. We need to use a bit of intuition and go through a process of rearrangement of the postcondition so we can see the appropriate statement to use.

The first thing we can notice in the postcondition is that $N == 1$ is a special case: when it is true we know immediately that N is not prime; if we know that $N > 1$, then there is more work to do. This sounds a lot like a selection based on a comparison of N and 1. If we focus on the comparisons of N and 1 we can convert the postcondition to the following form (see the explanation at the end of this section if you need convincing):

```
// Assert: ( N == 1 AND Answer == false) OR
//            ( N > 1   AND
//              (Answer == false  AND
//                There is I: 2 <= I < N AND N % I == 0 ) ) OR
//              ( Answer == true   AND
//                 For I = 2,...,N-1: N % I != 0 ) )
//           )
```

This rearrangement of the postcondition clearly shows the form we expect to see after a selection statement – more particularly, a one-way selection with default. (Notice that since the precondition states that $N > 0$, $N > 1$ is true if $N == 1$ is false.) We can replace `Statement` by the following code segment:

```
// Assert: N > 0

if (N == 1)
     Answer == false;
else // Assert: N >= 2  {

    Stmt

    // Assert: ( Answer == false AND
    //             There is I: 2 <= I < N AND N % I == 0 ) OR
    //           ( Answer == true   AND
    //             For I = 2,...,N-1: N % I != 0 )
}
```

Your first reaction now might be that `Stmt` should be another selection based on the value of `Answer`. But of course this is not possible since `Answer` does not have a value initially to select on – that value is what the algorithm is to determine! So `Stmt` must be a repetition statement. This doesn't come as a surprise since the only way to make a statement about all the values between 2 and N is by using repetition. Since the key to the semantics of repetition is the loop invariant, we just figure out a good candidate condition, then fill in the code, and show that the code will make the candidate true before every pass.

When `Stmt` terminates the value of `Answer` will be determined by whether there is a value between 2 and $N - 1$, which divides N. If and when we find a divisor in this range we will terminate the repetition and report that `Answer` is false. Then it would seem that a reasonable condition to try as the invariant is "no previous value divides N." This sounds good. Notice in the postcondition when `Answer` is true we make that exact statement, where "previous" is relative to N. Our invariant candidate will be the following:

```
For I = 2,...,Count-1: N % I != 0
```

At the same time it is clear that the invariant makes sense only as long as the value of `Count` doesn't exceed `N`. So we can also give the loop variant as `N-Count`, as a measure of progress through the repetition.

To define a repetition we need three elements: the initialization, the body, and the condition. We will determine the condition first. There are obviously two ways for the repetition to end – either we run through all possible divisors or find that `Answer` is false. Divisors will be exhausted when `Count == N` is true, so the following condition should be true when the loop terminates:

```
!Answer OR (Count == N)
```

If this is true when the loop terminates, then its opposite should be true if the loop is to be entered again. In other words, the loop condition should be

```
Answer AND (Count < N)
```

You might be tempted to conclude that `Answer == true` should be added to the loop invariant – but remember that at some point the value of `Answer` can become false and kick us out of the loop. So `Answer` is not always true when we reach the loop condition. This gives us the following form for the repetition:

```
// Assert: N >= 2

Init;
while // Variant:   N - Count >= 0
      // Invariant: For I = 2,...,Count-1: N % I != 0
      ( Answer && (Count < N) ) {
      S;
}
```

```
// Assert: ( Answer == false AND
//             There is I: 2 <= I < N AND N % I == 0 ) OR
//           ( Answer == true  AND
//             For I = 2,...,N-1: N % I != 0 )
```

The initialization is relatively easy. The invariant implies that starting `Count` at 2 is appropriate. If the invariant is to be believed, then we can also conclude that, at least based on the values checked so far, `N` is prime – i.e., a preliminary value of `Answer` should be true. So we should also initialize `Answer` to true.

```
// Assert: N >= 2

Count  = 2;
Answer = true;
while // Invariant: For I = 2,...,Count-1: N % I != 0
      ( Answer && (Count < N) ) {
      S;
}

// Assert: ( Answer == false AND
//             There is I: 2 <= I < N AND N % I == 0 ) OR
//           ( Answer == true  AND
//             For I = 2,...,N-1: N % I != 0 )
```

Well, we've saved the hard part till last. What statements should be in the loop body? By looking at the loop postcondition, the loop condition, and the invariant, we should be able to conclude what the body's postcondition should be. The only way the first clause of the loop's postcondition can be true is if the current value of `Count` is found to divide `N` – in this case the value of `Answer` must also be false. For the second clause of the postcondition to be true it must be that `Count` is equal to `N` and that `(pre)Count` is not a divisor of `N`. That's a bit quick! Remember that on entry to the loop body `Count < N` is true. If in the postcondition for the body `Count == N` is true, then the value of `Count` must have changed. So the body's postcondition can be stated as follows:

```
(N % (pre)Count == 0 AND Answer == false) OR
(N % (pre)Count != 0 AND Count = (pre)Count + 1)
```

Fortunately, we have seen this pattern before: the `OR` of two disjoint clauses points to an `if...then...else` construction as follows:

```
// Assert: Count < N AND Answer
if (N % Count == 0)
     Answer = false;
else // Assert: N % Count != 0
     Count = Count + 1;
// Assert: (N % (pre)Count == 0 AND
//           Answer == false)
```

```
//              OR
//         (N % (pre)Count != 0 AND
//            Count = (pre)Count + 1)
```

We seem to have succeeded in all we set out to do. Beginning with the pre- and postconditions defining the problem of determining primeness, we have worked our way backwards, at each point analyzing the current postcondition and determining what kind of statement will force that postcondition. The fully asserted final code for testing primeness is as follows:

```
// Assert: N > 0

if (N == 1)
     Answer = false;
else // Assert: N >= 2  {

     Count  = 2;
     Answer = true;
     while // Variant:   N - Count >= 0
          // Invariant: For I = 2,...,Count-1: N % I != 0
          ( Answer && (Count < N) ) {

          if (N % Count == 0)
               Answer = false;
          else
               Count = Count + 1;

          // Assert: (N % (pre)Count == 0 AND
          //             Answer == false)
          //           OR
          //          (N % (pre)Count != 0 AND
          //             Count = (pre)Count + 1)
     }

     // Assert: ( Answer == false AND
     //           There is I: 2 <= I < N AND N % I == 0 )
     //            OR
     //          ( Answer == true   AND
     //            For I = 2,...,N-1: N % I != 0 )
}

// Assert: ( Answer == false AND
//           ( N == 1          OR
//             There is I: 2 <= I < N AND N % I == 0 ) ) OR
//          ( Answer == true   AND
//            N > 1             AND
//            For I = 2,...,N-1: N % I != 0 )
```

Converting the Postcondition

Earlier in this section we claimed that in the following, condition A can be converted to the condition B. The demonstration follows:

Condition A:

```
// Assert: ( Answer == false AND
//            ( N == 1          OR
//              There is I: 2 <= I < N AND N % I == 0 ) )
//            OR
//          ( Answer == true   AND
//            N > 1             AND
//            For I = 2,...,N-1: N % I != 0 )
```

Condition B:

```
// Assert: ( N == 1 AND Answer == false) OR
//         ( N > 1   AND
//           (Answer == false  AND
//            There is I: 2 <= I < N AND N % I == 0 ) )
//               OR
//           ( Answer == true   AND
//             For I = 2,...,N-1: N % I != 0 ) )
//         )
```

To do a rearrangement it is easiest if we consider condition A to be in the form

```
(A AND (N == 1 OR C)) OR (A1 AND N > 1 AND C1)
```

where the letters stand in place of the obvious subexpressions. The left half of the expression can be converted as follows:

```
A AND (N == 1 OR C)

A AND (N == 1 OR (N != 1 AND C))
// see Example 1 in Appendix A

A AND (N == 1 OR (N > 1 AND C))
// since N > 0 is assumed

(A AND N == 1) OR (A AND N > 1 AND C)
// distribute AND
```

This transforms our postcondition into the following three-way OR (notice that the comparisons of N to 1 have been moved to the front):

```
(N == 1 AND A) OR (N > 1 AND A AND C) OR (N > 1 AND A AND C)
```

Now we can undistribute the N > 1 to get

(N == 1 AND A) OR (N > 1 AND ((A AND C) OR (A AND C)))

which can be converted back to get condition B.

```
// Assert: ( N == 1 AND Answer == false) OR
//            ( N > 1   AND
//                (Answer == false  AND
//                There is I: 2 <= I < N AND N % I == 0 ) )
//                     OR
//                ( Answer == true   AND
//                  For I = 2,...,N-1: N % I != 0 ) )
//            )
```

Lesson 13

More on Abstraction

Applying persuasive programming to abstractions is straightforward and doesn't really require a more in-depth look. But there is a particular type of abstraction which should be discussed – the recursive abstraction. Recursive abstractions are interesting, not because they require a new, more sophisticated persuasive approach — they don't — but because there is a close tie to the related mathematical concepts of *inductive definition* and *proof by mathematical induction*.

13.1   Recursion – An Overview

A *recursive* definition is one which defines something in terms of itself. In programming, an abstraction which contains a call to itself is referred to as a *recursive abstraction*. In imperative languages such as C^{++} recursion is a feature which is infrequently used but is essential in certain problem solutions.

Recursion is a general mechanism for repetition. In functional languages, such as lisp and ML and in logic programming languages, such as prolog, recursion is the only mechanism for repetition. In fact, C^{++} could do without its range of repetition structures by requiring all repetition to be done with recursive abstractions. A very simple example will suffice. Here are two C^{++} functions which implement the factorial function, one using the `while` statement and the other using recursion:

```
int factorial(int n) {                 int factorial(int n) {
    // Pre:  n >= 0                         // Pre:  n >= 0
    // Post: return n!                      // Post: return n!
    int fact = 1;                           int fact;
    int i = 2;                              if (n == 0) fact = 1;
    while (i <= n) {                        else
        fact = fact * i;                        fact = n*fact(n-1);
        i = i + 1;                          return fact;
    }                                   }
    return fact;
}
```

The definition on the left is similar to the other uses of repetition we have seen
in earlier examples. A side-by-side tracing of the execution of the two functions
will expose the essence of the recursive style – for the purposes of the trace we
will assume the call `factorial(3)`. The trace on the left is just an unwinding
of the loop. On the right, there is a sequence of calls, with the trace of each call
being indented.

```
n == 3                              n == 3
fact == 1 AND i == 2
// Assert: i <= 3                   // Assert: n > 1
fact == 1*2                         // call factorial(2)
i    == 3

// Assert: i <= 3                       n == 2
fact == 1*2*3                           // Assert: n > 1
i    == 4                               // call factorial(1)

// Assert: i > 4                            n == 1
return fact == 1*2*3                        // Assert: n == 1
                                            // call factorial(0)
                                                n == 0
                                                return fact == 1
                                            return  fact == 1*1
                                        return fact == 2*1*1
                                    return fact == 3*2*1*1
```

Notice a couple of things. First, the length of the recursive version is longer due
to more assertions in the trace. Second, notice in the recursive trace that the
calls to `factorial` are nested in the sense that a return from a call doesn't occur
until the inner call returns – thus the repetition. Also notice that the selection
condition turns out to control how long the recursion continues because when
it becomes true there is no additional call – we call it the "base case."

One of the very appealing characteristics of recursion in programming is its
close connection to induction in mathematics. Inductive definitions are quite
common in mathematics, with the most familiar being for the function we have

just been discussing – the factorial function.

$$x! = \begin{cases} 1 & \text{x} = 0, \\ x \times (\text{x-1})! & \text{x} > 0. \end{cases}$$

Another notation where the connection to induction may be less clear is the summation. The following inductive definition defines the notation:

$$\sum_{i=1}^{x} i = \begin{cases} 1 & \text{x} = 1, \\ x + \sum_{i=1}^{x-1} i & \text{x} > 1. \end{cases}$$

The two examples remind us that, as with recursion in programming, an inductive definition involves defining something in terms of itself and that there must be at least one base case. In the examples the base case is given by the first line of the definition and the inductive part is given by the second line. The parallel between the inductive and recursive definitions is hard to miss, but why do we care?

Mathematical induction is a proof technique associated with inductive definitions. Consider the following equality:

$$\sum_{i=1}^{x} i \;\; = \;\; x * (x+1)/2.$$

Is it true? Since we have an inductive definition of $\sum_{i=1}^{x} i$, we can use mathematical induction to prove the equality always holds (for all positive integers).

Base Case
If we substitute 1 for x in the equation we see that both sides of the equality reduce to 1. The equality holds for the base case of $x = 1$.

Induction Hypothesis
Assume that the equality holds for the integer value x.

Induction Case
Prove that the equality must hold for the value $x + 1$.

$$\sum_{i=1}^{x+1} i \;\; = \;\; (x+1) + \sum_{i=1}^{x} i$$
$$= \;\; (x+1) + x * (x+1)/2$$
$$= \;\; (x+1) * (1 + (x+1)/2) = ((x+1) * (x+2))/2.$$

So by mathematical induction the equality is true for all possible values of x.

One way to interpret the proof is as follows: if we want to see that the equality works for a particular integer value, we can start with the base case and work our way to the value in question, applying the definition at each step. This is exactly what happened in the trace of the recursive version of `factorial` above.

13.2   Asserting Recursive Abstractions

We want to be able to appropriately assert recursive abstractions. In the first
example of this lesson we looked at a recursive implementation of the factorial
function. The code there is typical of recursive abstractions – i.e., selection-
based rather than repetition-based and with at least one of the selection cases
lacking a call to the abstraction. The selection structure exactly matches the
form of inductive/recursive definitions. Consider our recursive implementation
of the factorial function:

```
int factorial(int n) {
    // Pre:   n >= 0
    // Post: return n!

    int fact;
    if (n == 0) fact = 1;                    // A
    else        fact = n*factorial(n-1);     // B
    // Assert: ( n == 0 AND fact == 1 ) OR
    //         ( n >  0 AND fact == n*factorial(n-1)
    return fact;
}
```

The postcondition which follows the selection statement is the natural consequence of the selection semantics we discussed in Lesson 6. But this postcondition is different from the abstraction postcondition. In fact, the abstraction
postcondition is an expectation and should really be replaced by the selection
postcondition. But there's another step we can take to make the abstraction
persuasive. The following implementation is the same except the abstraction
postcondition has been replaced by one which is clearly equivalent to the selection postcondition – "clearly" because it is just a syntactic alteration, with
factorial replacing fact and the selection conditions being pulled out to the
right.

```
int factorial(int n) {
    // Pre:   n >= 0
    // Post: factorial(n) = 1                 n == 0
    //                    = n*factorial(n-1)  n >  0

    int fact;
    if (n == 0) fact = 1;                    // A
    else        fact = n*factorial(n-1);     // B
    // Assert: ( n == 0 AND fact == 1 ) OR
    //         ( n >  0 AND fact == n*factorial(n-1)
    return fact;
}
```

One advantage of this particular rendition is that the postcondition is close in
structure to the usual mathematical definition for $n!$

Before going on to discuss recursion and ADTs, we look at two traditional but quite different examples of recursion: a function for computing the Fibonacci numbers and a function for sorting a list of integer values – *quicksort*.

Example 29 – Fibonacci numbers
▼

The value of the nth Fibonacci number can be defined as follows:

$$\text{fib}(n) = \begin{cases} 1 & n \leq 1, \\ \text{fib}(n-1) + \text{fib}(n-2) & n > 1. \end{cases}$$

Using this definition and following the lead for the factorial abstraction above, a C^{++} function for computing the nth Fibonacci number can be expressed as follows:

```
int fib(int n) {
     // Pre:  n >= 0
     // Post: Return the n-th Fibonacci number.

     int Answer;
     if (n <= 1) Answer = 1;
     else        Answer = fib(n - 1) + fib(n - 2);

     return Answer;
}
```

Again, we have initially placed a postcondition which expresses our expectations rather than reflecting any analysis of the code. But this abstraction yields to analysis just as easily as the one above. The postcondition for the selection statement follows easily from the work in Lesson 6.

```
if (n <= 1) Answer = 1;
else            Answer = fib(n - 1) + fib(n - 2);
// Assert: (n <= 1 AND Answer == 1) OR
//         (n >  1 AND Answer == fib(n-1) + fib(n-2))
```

Again, this postcondition reflects the inductive definition which appears above, so we will adopt the inductive definition for our postcondition just as we did with the factorial function. Again we make use of the slight rearrangement style from the factorial function.

```
int fib(int n) {
     // Pre:  n >= 0
     // Post: fib (n) == 1                      n <= 1
     //                == fib(n-2) + fib(n-1)   n >= 2
```

```
        int Answer;
        if (n <= 1) Answer = 1;
        else        Answer = fib(n - 1) + fib(n - 2);
        // Assert: (n <= 1 AND Answer == 1) OR
        //          (n >  1 AND Answer ==
        //                           fib(n-1) + fib(n-2))

        return Answer;
    }
```

▲

Example 30 – Quicksort
▼

Sorting a list of data is not an inherently recursive process, so when we consider the quicksort algorithm, we should not expect to see a recursive definition as we did with `fib`. Instead, we will use the connection between recursion and mathematical induction to show that the algorithm below is correct.

The idea behind quicksort is to repeatedly split the list "in half" and recursively sort each "half." The word "half" is quoted because the process of splitting doesn't have to guarantee an even split – in fact it is possible to produce one "half" which is empty! Notice that in this description, the recursion appears in a slightly different way. In the previous two examples, and in following examples, the recursive structure is one element followed by the rest of the structure. But in quicksort we have two lists and are guaranteed that each list is shorter than the original. Thus we can argue inductively and be guaranteed that the recursion (process of splitting in half) will eventually end.

Here is the algorithm written out. We'll assume for simplicity that the list is maintained in an array and that the elements are integer values:

```
void Qsort(int list[], int first, int last) {
    // Pre:  0 <= first <= last <= maxElements
    //          AND
    //       For I = first,...,last:
    //          list[I] has a value
    // Post: (out)list is a permutation of (in)list
    //       For I = first,...,last-1:
    //          (out)list[I] <= (out)list[I+1]

    if (first < last) {
        int psn;
```

```
        split(list, first, last, psn);
        // Assert: list is a permutation of (pre)list
        //          AND
        //          For I = first,...,psn-1:
        //              list[I] < list[psn]
        //          AND
        //          For I = psn+1,...,last:
        //              list[I] >= list[psn]

        Qsort(list, first, psn-1);
        Qsort(list, psn+1, last);
    }

}
```

The use of the *permutation* is important here. When we sort a
list we should claim, at the end, that the (out) list has the same
elements as the (in) list, though they may be in a different order.
This is exactly the meaning of permutation – two lists which are the
same except for ordering. Unfortunately, the Boolean expression
which expresses this condition is extremely complex and long. So,
since the idea is clear, we use a name for the condition rather than
writing the expression.

The question, of course, is whether the inherent semantics of `Qsort`
is the same as the intended semantics. Though proof by induction
is not exactly in the scope of this text, we will use it anyway to
prove that this quicksort implementation is correct. We make one
assumption in advance: the abstraction `split` will always split a list
of two or more elements, as described by the assertion following the
call, by situating an element (the pivot) in the list and rearranging
the other elements of the list so that every element before the pivot
is less than the pivot and every element following the pivot is greater
than or equal to the pivot.

The induction argument is slightly different in this case as compared
to the argument given above for the summation equality, but the idea
is the same.

Base Case

> If the condition (`first == last`) is true, then since
> there is only one element in this part of the list, it is
> sorted!

Induction Hypothesis

> Any list of length less than `last-first+1` is correctly
> sorted by `Qsort`.

Induction Case

Prove that `list` from position `first` to `last` is sorted by `Qsort`.

We have assumed that the abstraction `split` works correctly. In that case each time we call `Qsort`, the list to be sorted will be shorter by at least one element than the original part of the list. This is because the split element is not considered in either split part – in fact it is in its correct position in the list and will never have to be moved again.

The induction hypothesis then says that both of these lists will be correctly sorted by `Qsort`. Then the following conditions are true:

```
(out)list[first...psn-1] is a
        permutation of (in)list[first...psn-1] AND
For I = first,...,psn-1: list[I] < list[psn] AND
For I = first,...,psn-2: list[I] <= list[I+1]

(out)list[psn+1...last] is a
        permutation of (in)list[psn+1...last] AND
For I = psn+1,...,last: list[psn] <= list[I] AND
For I = psn+1,...,last-1: list[I] <= list[I+1]
```

But this clearly implies the following condition is true

```
(out)list[first...last] is a permutation of
    (in)list[first...last] AND
For I = first,...,last-1: list[I] <= list[I+1]
```

So by induction, the quicksort algorithm must correctly sort all vectors.

▲

In this last example we have used the induction connection, not to provide a mathematical definition or to more effectively assert the code, but to supply the proof method which has allowed us to prove `Qsort` correct. Again at the heart of both examples is the notion that we can work backwards to a base case and then work in reverse order to construct the desired result. This is the essence of recursion.

13.3   Recursive Data Structures

The previous example uncovers a connection between data and recursion. Just as the summation can be defined recursively,

$$\sum_{i=1}^{x} i = \begin{cases} 1 & x = 1, \\ x + \sum_{i=1}^{x-1} i & x > 1, \end{cases}$$

so can data structures be defined recursively. For example, we can define a list recursively as follows:

$$\text{list} = \begin{cases} [\,] \\ x \oplus \text{list} \end{cases}$$

The operation $\oplus$ is just a notation for denoting a list as an element x along with "the rest of the list." The circle around the plus is just to avoid confusion with the arithmetic operation. This definition says that a list is either the empty list, [ ], or some element along with the rest of the list. Of course, it is inherent in the recursive definition that "the rest of the list" is itself a list and is either empty or is an element along with the rest of the list. If we consider lists of integers, then we can describe the list containing the first three integer values as

$$3 \oplus (2 \oplus (1 \oplus [\,])).$$

Recursion on a List

This definition of list is very abstract – i.e., there is no clear connection between the definition and a particular implementation of a list structure. If, for example, we consider a list structure to be an initial segment of an array along with a variable `length` to hold the length of the list, then the $\oplus$ operation could be interpreted as the last element in the array along with the part of the array preceding the last element.

Having defined a recursive structure for the list, we can implement new operations based on that structure. A simple example is to determine the number of list elements which have a particular property – let's say we want to know the number of positive values. According to the recursive structure, we should get a count from the recursive portion of the list and then, if the last element is positive, increment the count. The base case of the recursion, of course, would be to report 0 as the count for the empty list. Here is a C^{++} function that implements this simple operation:

```
void countPos(int list[], int len) {
    // Pre:  len >= 0 AND
    //       For I = 0,...,len-1: list[I] has a value
    // Post:

    if (len == 0)    // Assert: the base case
        count = 0;
    else {           //         the recursive case
        count = countPos(list, len-1);
        if (list[len-1] > 0) count = count + 1;
    }
    // Assert: ( len == 0 AND count == 0 ) OR
    //         ( len >  0 AND
    //            ( (list[len-1] >  0 AND
```

```
//              count == countPos(list, len-1) + 1)
//                  OR
//              (list[len-1] <= 0 AND
//                  count == countPos(list, len-1))
//              )
//          ) AND return count
    return count;
}
```

The complex selection postcondition follows naturally from the Lesson 6 work.
If we think of the recursive definitions for factorial and fib functions, we see
that a similar option for transforming the abstraction postcondition is available.
In fact, we can complete the postcondition as follows:

```
void cPos(int list[], int len) {
    // Pre:  len >= 0 AND
    //       For I = 0,...,len-1: list[I] has a value
    // Post: cPos(list, len) = 0
    //           len = 0;
    //         = cPos(list[0...len-2], len-1):
    //             list[len-1] <= 0
    //         = 1+cPos(list[0...len-2], len-1)
    //             list[len-1] >  0

    if (len == 0)   // Assert: the base case
        count = 0;
    else {          //          the recursive case
        count = cPos(list, len-1);
        if (list[len-1] > 0) count = count + 1;
    }
    // Assert: ( len == 0 AND count == 0 ) OR
    //         ( len >  0 AND
    //           ( (list[len-1] >  0 AND
    //               count == cPos(list, len-1) + 1)
    //                 OR
    //             (list[len-1] <= 0 AND
    //               count == cPos(list, len-1))
    //           )
    //         ) AND return count
    return count;
}
```

Another more complex list operation is for inserting a new element into a
sorted list so the resulting list is still sorted. According to our recursive definition
of a list there are two cases to consider:

Base

> If the list is empty, then adding a new element in order just means putting the element at position 0 and setting the list length to 1.

Recursive

> Here we know that there is an initial list followed by the last element. Since we want the element to be added in order, we have two cases to worry about:
>
> - The new element is greater than the last element: in this case make the new element the last element in the resulting list and increment the list length.
> - The new element is not greater than the last element: we make the original last element the last element of the resulting list and then *insert our element in the initial part of the list.*

By following the recursive definition we don't have to worry about loops or their variants and invariants – we let the recursion take care of that. The following C^{++} function implements this design:

```
void insert(int n, int list[], int & len) {
    // Pre:  n has a value AND len >= 0 AND
    //       For I = 0,...,len-2: list[I] <= list[I+1]
    // Post: (out)len == (in)len + 1 AND
    //       There is I: 0 <= I <= (in)len
    //           AND
    //             For J = 0,...,I-1:
    //                 (out)list[J] == (in)list[J] AND
    //             (out)list[I] == n
    //                 AND
    //             For J = I+1,...,(in)len:
    //                 (out)list[J] == (in)list[J-1])

    if (len == 0) // Assert: the empty list case
        list[0] = n;
    else          // Assert: list[len-1] + rest of list
        if (n >= list[len-1]) { // Assert: n belongs at
                                //            the end
            list[len] = n;
        else {  // Assert: n < list[len-1]
            //            insert it in the
            //            initial segment
            list[len] = list[len-1];
            int k = len - 1;
            // just to act as the reference param
```

```
                insert(n, list, k);
            }
        }
        len = len + 1;
    }
```

13.4   Pointer-based Recursive Structures

While the array is a common implementation mechanism for the list structure, it is not always appropriate. There are many other data structures, e.g., trees and graphs, for which the array is also an inappropriate implementation mechanism. For these data structures we rely on the ability to define structure components and link the structures together to reflect the form of the data structure. In C^{++} the linking mechanism is the *address type*, better known as a *pointer type*. In the rest of this section we will investigate the recursive nature of certain pointer-based data structures – in particular binary trees and linked lists.

Binary Trees

Another common recursive structure is the *binary tree*, where the structure is considered to be either empty or to have a base element, usually referred to as the *root*, with two trees attached, one on the left and the other on the right. The right tree, also called the `right subtree`, can be empty or be a root with left and right subtrees. The root of a subtree is usually referred to as a *node* of the whole tree. Those nodes for which both subtrees are empty are called *leaf nodes*. Here is a diagram that represents the structure of a tree:

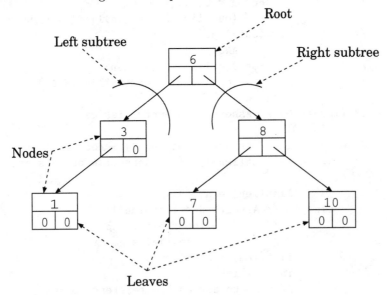

In C^{++} the typical implementation declares a node type and makes use of the *pointer* type to connect the nodes into the tree structure. Remember that a variable of a pointer type holds memory addresses and, consequently, can be used to link one structure to another. Here is a typical type definition for a tree node:

```
TreeNode struct {
                int value;
                TreeNode * rtree;
                TreeNode * ltree;
            } * tree;
```

Here the variable `tree` can hold the address of a node – in particular of a root node. If `tree` has value NULL, then `tree` represents the empty tree. But the following sequence of code results in a tree with two subtrees.

```
TreeNode * treeR;
TreeNode * treeL;
... // code where treeR and treeL are built
tree = new TreeNode;
tree.value = 25;
tree.rtree = treeR;
tree.ltree = treeL;
```

This description, of course, is also recursive since the way that `tree` is constructed must be repeated within the "code where `treeR` and `treeL` are built."

Having defined the structure of an `int` tree we can now take a look at the implementation of a tree operation, namely, the operation that determines the sum of all the values stored in the tree. This tree sum is 0 if the tree is empty and the sum of the value at the root node plus the sums from the left and right subtrees if the tree is not empty. Again, the recursive structure of the data type is reflected in the implementation.

```
int treeSum(TreeNode * t) {
    // Pre:  t == NULL OR
    //       (t->) has a TreeNode value
    // Post: ???
    int sum;
    if (t == NULL)
        sum = 0;
    else // Assert: t-> has a TreeNode value
        sum = t->value +
                treeSum(t->rtree) +
                treeSum(t->ltree);
    // Assert: (t == NULL AND sum == 0) OR
    //         (t != NULL AND
    //          sum == t->value + t->ltree + t->rtree)
    return sum;
}
```

The postcondition is clearly correct based on our understanding of selection semantics, but again, since this is a function returning a value, we should be able to write the abstraction postcondition in the form of a recursive function definition. Here is the easy transformation:

```
int treeSum(TreeNode * t) {
    // Pre:  t == NULL OR
    //       (t->) has a TreeNode value
    // Post: treeSum(t) == 0                        t == NULL
    //                 == t->value +
    //                       treeSum(t->ltree) +
    //                       treeSum(t->rtree)      t != NULL

    int sum;
    if (t == NULL)
        sum = 0;
    else // Assert: t-> has a TreeNode value
        sum = t->value +
              treeSum(t->rtree) +
              treeSum(t->ltree);
    // Assert: (t == NULL AND sum == 0) OR
    //         (t != NULL AND sum ==
    //              t->value + treeSum(t->rtree) +
    //              treeSum(t->ltree))

    return sum;
}
```

Linked Lists

Earlier in this section we looked at examples involving lists that were implemented using arrays. But there are times when using an array to implement a list is not appropriate, and in this case we implement the list as a sequence of nodes linked by single pointer values. Pointer-based lists are called *linked lists*. Here is how we could define a simple list node:

```
ListNode struct {
            int value;
            ListNode * next;
        } * list;
```

The variable list can hold the address of a node. As with the tree structure, an empty list is represented by setting list to NULL, while otherwise list will have a value which is the address of a ListNode. That node, which we say is at the head of the list, can have its next value either set to NULL or to point to another node. If we start at the head of a list we can follow next values until we find the last node of the list, whose next value is required to be NULL.

Notice that this structure exactly matches the recursive definition of list we gave earlier.

The implementation of list operations is not very different from the array-based versions. The one difference is that it becomes convenient to think of the recursive structure as being the first element followed by the rest of the list, whereas in the array-based implementation we thought of the list as an element (the last one) preceded by the rest of the list.

We will look at the re-implementation of the `insert` function for the pointer-based lists, but there is a notational problem to deal with first. In the array-based implementation we relied heavily on array syntax to allow us to write conditions about a list. With pointer-based lists we do not have such a convenient notation. Instead we will go back to the notation we have used for input streams. Since we are dealing with sequences of values we will denote pointer-based lists as follows:

<t1,...,tn> for a list of length $n > 0$ and
< > for the empty list

Using the notation just described, here is a function that implements the `insert` operation:

```
void insert(int n, NodeType * list, int & len) {
    // Pre:  n has a value AND len >= 0 AND
    //       list == <t1,...,t(len)>      AND
    //       For I = 1,...,len-1: tI <= t(I+1)
    // Post: (out)len == (in)len + 1           AND
    //       (out)list == <s1,...,s((out)len)> AND
    //       There is I: 1 <= I <= (in)len     AND
    //             For J = 1,...,I-1: sJ == tJ AND
    //             sI == n                      AND
    //             For J = I+1,...,(in)len: sJ == t(J-1)

    if (list == NULL) { // Assert: the empty list case
        list = new ListNode;
        list->value = n;
        list->next = NULL;
    }
    else {              // Assert: t1 + rest of list
        if (n < list->value) {
            // Assert: n belongs at the beginning
            ListNode N = new ListNode;
            N->value = n;
            N->next = list;
            list = N;
        }
```

```
            else { // Assert: n >= list->value
                 //           insert it in the
                 //              rest of the list
                 int k = len-1;
                   // just to be the reference param
                 insert(n, list->next, k);
            }
       }
       len = len + 1;
   }
```

The algorithm is different in the details, but not in the structure. The detail differences are the storage of the inserted value in the node and also the linking of the node to the rest of the list.

Lesson 14

Are You Persuaded?

Early in this series of lessons we expressed the desire to be able to deduce a precise postcondition for a complete program for which we have a precondition. The process of persuasive programming, which you have studied in these lessons, can be used to produce such a postcondition. The derived postcondition, representing the inherent semantics of the program, can be compared to the original postcondition, which represents the intended semantics. If they are the same we are confident that the program is correct. We summarize this idea in the following definition.

Program Verification

If the precondition for a program is satisfied, then

1. the postcondition for the program is satisfied *and*

2. the program is guaranteed to halt.

The process just described, applying assertions after the program is written, is not the only option. Sometimes a required postcondition gives a strong hint as to the structure of the code which should be written. This process of deriving code from a postcondition is very powerful, and when properly applied leads to a program that is correct. A middle ground mixes the two processes, deducing statements when possible and otherwise generating statements intuitively, verifying them after the fact. The two examples that follow illustrate these ideas:

14.1   A Guessing Game Program

For our first example we will take an already-written program and assert it in order to determine the inherent semantics. The program we will assert implements a traditional guessing game in which one player thinks of a target value between two bounds (say 1 and 100) and then the other player sees how many tries it takes to guess the target. With each try the player is told either that the guess is correct or that the target is greater or less than the guess. The idea, of course, is to play the game many times, alternating guessers, to see which player requires the lowest number of guesses (on average). Here is a complete program that implements the game:

```
void GetBounded(String prompt, int L, int H, int& V) {
  cout << prompt << " between " << L
              << " and " << H << " >> ";
  cin >> V;
  while ((V < L) || (V > H)) {
    cout << " between " << L
        << " and " << H << " >> ";
    cin >> V;
  }
}

void Guess(int L, int H, int target, int& guesses) {
  int guessed;
  GetBounded("Enter guess", L, H, guessed);
  guesses = 1;
  while (guessed != target) {
    if (guessed > target)
          H = guessed-1;
    else L = guessed+1;
    GetBounded("Enter guess", L, H, guessed);
    guesses = guesses + 1;
  }
}

void main() {
  int low = 1, hi = 100;
  int target;
  int guesses;
  GetBounded("Enter target", low, hi, target);
  Guess(low, hi,  target, guesses);
  cout << "It took " << guesses
      << " to guess the target " << target
      << endl;
}
```

Are you persuaded? Does this program look as though it implements the game described? It may look like a good attempt and maybe you can't see any immediate problems, but would you absolutely guarantee the program? Probably not, if for no other reason than the fact that the loop in Guess with the selection statement looks like it could be a source of tricky problems.

So where should we start? We have a clear choice between starting with the main and working inward to the abstractions, or starting with the abstractions and working outward to main. Since we are interested in actual semantics, it would seem that starting in the functions would be the best bet. In this way we can determine interfaces for the abstractions, based on their inherent semantics, and then apply those when we analyze the code for main.

We will begin with GetBounded, since it is called in both Guess and main. Then we will turn our attention to Guess and finally to main. In the end we should have a precondition and a postcondition for the program.

Asserting GetBounded

The code in the function GetBounded looks very much like the repetition statement that we analyzed in Lesson 7.4. In the current situation we have an abstraction of that repetition code. The tricky bit is trying to understand what the precondition should be, but the code contains hints.

GetBounded clearly accesses both the standard input and output streams. The input stream must contain some unknown amount of data since there is an indefinite loop at the heart of the code. Also, if the loop body is to ever execute, it must be the case that L <= H. So we can begin

```
void GetBounded(String prompt, int L, int H, int& V) {
    // Pre:  L <= H AND
    //       input stream == <v1,...,vn,...>
    // Post: ???

    cout << prompt << " between " << low
                   << " and " << hi << " >> ";
    cin >> V;

    while ((V < L) || (V > H)) {
        cout << " between " << low
             << " and " << hi << " >> ";
        cin >> V;
    }
}
```

Having a partial precondition will allow us to deduce the semantics of the code. An execution of the code (an unwinding) will consume consecutive values from the input stream, only stopping when a value between the values of L and H is input. But this means that whenever we reach the test of the loop condition, all

previous input values have fallen outside the interval defined by L and H. The
loop variant should be obvious.

```
void GetBounded(String prompt, int L, int H, int& V) {
    // Pre:  L <= H AND
    //       input stream == <v1,...,vn>
    // Post: ???

    cout << prompt << " between " << low
                   << " and " << hi << " >> ";
    cin >> V;

    while // Variant: n - (R) - 1 >= 0
         // Invariant:
         //     For I = 1,...,(R):
         //         vI < L AND vI > H AND
         //     V == v((R)+1)
         ((V < L) || (V > H)) {
        cout << " between " << low
             << " and " << hi << " >> ";
        cin >> V; // Assert: variant decreases here!
    }
    // Assert: For I = 1,...,n-1: vI < L AND vI > H AND
    //         V == vn AND
    //         L <= V <= H
}
```

The loop postcondition, which follows naturally from the form of the loop's invariant and variant, also gives us a bit more information about the precondition
and, of course, the abstraction's postcondition. We learn about the precondition that the values on the input stream all satisfy the loop condition except
the final value, which falls between L and H. We arrive at the following inherent
semantics for GetBounded:

```
void GetBounded(String prompt, int L, int H, int& V) {
    // Pre:  L <= H                                      AND
    //       input stream == <v1,...,vn>                 AND
    //       For I = 1,...,n-1: vI < L AND vI > H AND
    //       L <= vn <= H
    // Post: input stream == <> AND
    //       (out)V == vn        AND
    //       L <= (out)V <= H

    cout << prompt << " between " << low
                   << " and " << hi << " >> ";
    cin >> V;
```

```
    while // Variant: n - (R) - 1 >= 0
          // Invariant:
          //     For I = 1,...,(R): vI < L AND vI > H
          //         AND
          //     V == v((R)+1)
          ((V < L) || (V > H)) {
          cout << " between " << low
               << " and " << hi << " >> ";
          cin >> V; // Assert: variant decreases here!
    }
    // Assert: For I = 1,...,n-1:
    //             vI < L AND vI > H
    //                 AND
    //         V == vn AND
    //         L <= V <= H
}
```

Asserting Guess

As with GetBounded, we must first determine what we can about the precondition for Guess. We know from a glance at the code in main and our analysis of GetBounded that the three parameters L, H, and target satisfy the condition L <= target <= H. In addition, since GetBounded is called in Guess, there must be a number of values on the input stream which will be consumed during the execution of Guess. We arrive at the following partial interface for Guess:

```
void Guess(int L, int H, int target, int& guesses)
    // Pre:  L <= target <= H              AND
    //       input stream == <v1,...,vn>   AND
    //       ???
    // Post: ???
```

The body of Guess is a loop structure in which GetBounded is repeatedly called to obtain a new value of guessed. If we perform an unwinding we should arrive at an understanding of the code semantics.

Here is the code of interest. Assertions have been added to the code to reflect what we know as a result of the analysis of GetBounded. We make use of the variable G rather than the hidden variable (R):

```
// Assert: input stream == <v1,...,vn>
GetBounded("Enter guess", L, H, guessed);
// Assert: input stream == <v2,...,vn>
//         L <= guessed == v1 <= H AND
//         L <= target <= H
G = 1;
while (guessed != target) {
    if (guessed > target)
```

```
            H = guessed-1;
      else L = guessed+1;
      // Assert: input stream == <v(G+1),...,vn>
      GetBounded("Enter guess", L, H, guessed);
      // Assert: input stream == <v(G+1),...,vn>
      //          L <= guessed == vG <= H AND
      //          L <= target <= H
      G = G + 1;
   }
```

There is another point to make here before going on. The assertions above indicate that the input stream contains n values, all of which seem to be valid from the point of view of GetBounded. For the purposes of clarity we are ignoring the invalid values which may be entered by the user. We relegate that detail to GetBounded and view the input stream in Guess at this more abstract, ideal level.

Looking at the loop in Guess we can see that loop body is straightforward except for the selection statement. We will look at an unwinding of the loop with the selection replaced by statement for the moment.

```
      // Assert: input stream == <v1,...,vn>
      GetBounded("Enter guess", L, H, guessed);
      // Assert: input stream == <v2,...,vn>
      //          L <= guessed == v1 <= H AND
      //          L <= target <= H          ******
      G = 1;

      // Assert: guessed != target        <<<---
      statement;
      // Assert: input stream == <v(G+1),...,vn>
      GetBounded("Enter guess", L, H, guessed);
      // Assert: input stream == <v(G+2),...,vn>
      //          L <= guessed == vG <= H
      G = G + 1;

      // Assert: guessed != target        <<<---
      statement;
      // Assert: input stream == <v(G+1),...,vn>
      GetBounded("Enter guess", L, H, guessed);
      // Assert: input stream == <v(G+2),...,vn>
      //          L <= guessed == vG <= H
      G = G + 1;

      // Assert: guessed != target        <<<---
      statement;
      // Assert: input stream == <v(G+1),...,vn>
      GetBounded("Enter guess", L, H, guessed);
```

```
// Assert: input stream == <v(G+2),...,vn>
//         L <= guessed == vG <= H
G = G + 1;


// Assert: guessed == target      <<<---
```

Notice that the condition labeled ****** disappears from the assertions that follow. This is because there's no guarantee that statement will maintain the truth of the condition – we know that statement alters one of L or H. Before continuing, then, we should work out the effect of statement on this unwinding.

We know for sure that the first time entering the loop and just before statement is to be executed, the condition

```
L <= target, guessed <= H AND
target != guessed
```

is true because it is guaranteed by the call to GetBounded and the success of the loop condition. We want to know whether statement maintains the truth of this condition. We can verify that it does by applying what we know of selection semantics. The following asserted code results:

```
// Assert: L <= target, guessed <= H AND
//         target != guessed       AND
//         L < H
if (guessed > target)
    H = guessed-1;
else L = guessed+1;
// Assert: ( (guessed > target AND H == guessed-1) OR
//           (guessed < target AND L == guessed+1) ) AND
//         L <= H
```

Since target and guessed don't change as a result of statement we know that the second clause of the precondition remains true, but what about the first and third clauses? A bit of simple math shows that the first clause does remain true. If L isn't changed by statement, then the new value of H is guessed-1 and, since guessed is greater than target, H is still greater than or equal to target. Similarly, if H remains unchanged by statement, the new value of L is guaranteed to be less than or equal to target. But we can no longer guarantee that L < H – only that L <= H. So, since the call to GetBounded doesn't change the values of L and H, we can modify the unwinding to reflect this new condition.

```
// Assert: input stream == <v1,...,vn>
GetBounded("Enter guess", L, H, guessed);
// Assert: input stream == <v2,...,vn>
//         L <= guessed == v1 <= H AND
//         L <= target <= H
G = 1;
```

```
// Assert: guessed != target        <<<---
statement;
// Assert: input stream == <v(G+1),...,vn>
GetBounded("Enter guess", L, H, guessed);
// Assert: input stream == <v(G+2),...,vn>
//          L <= guessed == vG <= H AND
//          L <= target <= H
G = G + 1;


// Assert: guessed != target        <<<---
statement;
// Assert: input stream == <v(G+1),...,vn>
GetBounded("Enter guess", L, H, guessed);
// Assert: input stream == <v(G+2),...,vn>
//          L <= guessed == vG <= H AND
//          L <= target <= H
G = G + 1;


// Assert: guessed != target        <<<---
statement;
// Assert: input stream == <v(G+1),...,vn>
GetBounded("Enter guess", L, H, guessed);
// Assert: input stream == <v(G+2),...,vn>
//          L <= guessed == vG <= H AND
//          L <= target <= H
G = G + 1;


// Assert: guessed == target        <<<---
```

We want a condition that is true every time before the loop condition is checked – the assertions marked with <<<---. Having read this unwinding earlier in this section we can clearly say that the following condition is an invariant of the loop:

```
input stream == <v(G+1),...,vn> AND
For I = 1,...,G-1: vI != target AND
L <= guessed == vG <= H          AND
L <= target <= H
```

If we take the natural deduction from this loop invariant, then we can deduce the following asserted loop:

```
// Assert: input stream == <v1,...,vn>
GetBounded("Enter guess", L, H, guessed);
G = 1;
while // Invariant: input stream == <v(G+1),...,vn>
     //            L <= guessed == vG <= H AND
```

```
       //                 L <= target <= H
       (guessed != target) {
       if (guessed > target)
            H = guessed-1;
       else L = guessed+1;
       GetBounded("Enter guess", L, H, guessed);
       G = G + 1;
  }
  // Assert: input stream == <>                      AND
  //         For I = 1,...,n-1: vI != target AND
  //         target == vn                            AND
  //         G == n
```

But what about the loop variant? How do we know that this loop has to terminate? The answer to this question is also tied up in the analysis of **statement** that we have just completed. That analysis indicates that after each execution of **statement** either H has decreased or L has increased, but they are still in the same order. And since we know that **target** is always between the two values, if the player is really a poor guesser, eventually the values L, H, and **target** will be the same. In that case, **target** will be the only value that GetBounded will allow to be returned. All of this means that the execution of the loop generates a sequence of nested intervals that decrease in size. The variant we adopt for the loop, then, is H - L. And we know that since this will eventually reach 0, the loop must terminate.

```
   void Guess(int L, int H, int target, int& G)
       // Pre:  L <= target <= H                 AND
       //       input stream == <v1,...,vn>      AND
       //       For I = 1,...,n-1: vI != target AND
       //       target == vn
       // Post: input stream == <> AND
       //       (out)G == n
   {
     GetBounded("Enter guess", L, H, guessed);
     G = 1;
     while // Variant: H >= L
          // Invariant: input stream == <v(G+1),...,vn>
          //            L <= guessed == vG <= H AND
          //            L <= target <= H
          (guessed != target) {
          if (guessed > target)
               H = guessed-1;
          else L = guessed+1;
          GetBounded("Enter guess", L, H, guessed);
          G = G + 1;
     }
   }
```

Asserting `main`

Well, the hard work has been done. We have determined an interface for each of the abstractions, and the code in `main` is really very easy to assert. We just need to make an instance of each interface (at least the relevant parts) at the sites of the calls, and we are done. The program apparently does what it was sold as doing. But at least now we have the solution written in persuasive code:

```
void main() {
  // pre:  input stream == <t,g1,...,gn> AND
  //       output stream == <>          AND
  //       1 <= t <= 100                AND
  //       For I = 1,...,n-1: vI != t    AND
  //       gn == target
  // post: input stream == <> AND
  //       G == n                 AND
  //       output stream ==
  //          <"It took <n> to guess the target <t>">

  int low = 1, hi = 100;
  int target;
  int G;

  // Assert: 1 == low <= hi == 100 AND
  //         input stream == <t,g1,...,gn>
  GetBounded("Enter target", low, hi, target);
  // Assert: low <= target == t <= hi
  //         input stream == <g1,...,gn>
  Guess(low, hi,  target, G);
  // Assert: input stream == <> AND
  //         G == n

  cout << "It took " << G
       << " to guess the target " << target
       << endl;
}
```

14.2   The Problem – Printing Primes

For the second problem we take a different tack – we take a specification of the problem and then, working backwards, generate the program that solves the problem.

The Problem

Write a program which first prompts the user for a *positive* input integer. As long as the user inputs an invalid number, the program will continue to prompt the user for an input value. In response to a valid input value, say N, the program will print the first N prime numbers and then stop.

Based on this description we will generate a program by first formalizing the specification into pre- and postconditions and then working backwards from the postcondition to determine the required program statements.

User Semantics

We begin by specifying the program's user semantics in the form of program pre- and postconditions. The postcondition is pretty clear – the output contains a finite list of consecutive primes starting from 2 (we'll see about being a bit more precise with this in a moment). But what about the precondition? Certainly the output stream is initially empty. But in analyzing a program we must have a way to specify the input. Though there is to be only one *valid* input value, it can be preceded by any number (including zero) of invalid values. The following is an appropriate specification of this condition:

```
input stream  = <v1,...,vN> AND
For I = 1,...,N-1: vI <= 0  AND
vN > 0                      AND
output stream == empty
```

Now, having clearly specified the precondition, we return our attention to the postcondition. The postcondition must indicate the input stream to be empty, but what about the output stream? The final output stream is really in two parts. The second part is a list of the first vN prime numbers. But what of the first part? Well, the first part is just the record of the program's side of the input dialog with the user. It will consist of N copies of the input prompt – the first N-1 of these prompts were followed by the user entering an invalid value, the final prompt was followed by the user entering a valid value vN. How should we specify this output stream? The most important thing is to be precise without being silly. Here is one possibility:

```
input stream  == empty
   AND
output stream ==
        Input a positive integer value >>
         .
         .  repeated N times
         .
        Input a positive integer value >>

        p1
         .
         .
```

```
                pvN
      AND
  p1,...,pvN are the first vN prime numbers
```

That's all right, but the last line says a lot. In some ways this last line is just
fine. It tells us just what to expect – and we'll know if it is right. But one reason
for being more precise is because the precision often directs us to an appropriate
algorithm. Here is a more precise way of saying the last line above. This could
also be improved on if we wanted to include the definition of prime:

```
  p1 == 2 is prime AND
  For I = 1,...,vN-1: p(I+1) is prime    AND
                      For K = pI+1,...,p(I+1)-1:
                                    K is not prime
```

Okay! This is a lot to write down just to say there is a list of the first vN
primes preceded by N input prompts. But it is only through precision we can be
sure our programs are correct. Remember that these simple programs improve
your skill, so when more difficult programs come along in the future you will be
sure you are writing the required program.

The Program – In Terms of Abstractions

At the most abstract level our program is supposed to get valid user input and
then print the required number of prime numbers. At the end the postcondition
must be true. We will focus on the postcondition to see if we get a hint as to
the code which should be included.

The postcondition seems to fall naturally into two parts – the input of the
valid integer value and the printing of the list of primes. If we allocate each of
these two actions to a separate abstraction, then it will be easy to determine the
pre- and postconditions for the abstractions. Here is the structure that results
from this simple analysis:

```
  int main () {

      int NumPrimes;   // the number of primes to be printed

      // Assert: input stream == <v1,...,vN>    AND
      //         For I = 1,...,v(N-1): vI <= 0 AND
      //         vN > 0

      GetPositive(NumPrimes);

      // Assert: input stream == empty AND
      //         NumPrimes == vN > 0    AND
      //         output stream ==
```

```
        //                    N copies of the input prompt


        PrintPrimes(NumPrimes);

        // Assert: input stream == empty AND
        //         NumPrimes == vN         AND
        //         output stream ==
        //                 N copies of the input prompt
        //
        //                 p1
        //                  .
        //                  .
        //                  .
        //                 pvN        AND
        //         p1 == 2 is prime AND
        //         For I = 1,...,vN-1:
        //             p(I+1) is prime    AND
        //             For K = pI+1,...,p(I+1)-1:
        //                 K is not prime
    }
```

And, of course, what we know is before the call to GetPositive the program precondition is true and after the call to PrintPrimes the program postcondition is true. In fact, the first call will produce the first half of the output and the second call will produce the second half. So our postcondition for the call to GetPositive (and, consequently, the precondition for the call to PrintPrimes) must assert that the input stream is empty, NumPrimes has a value (vN, in fact), and the output stream has N copies of the input prompt.

Now we just have to implement the two abstractions so that their inherent semantics match the intended semantics as represented by the postconditions above.

Expanding the Abstractions

So far we have a correct program written in terms of the new (abstract) operations GetPositive and PrintPrimes. We know what we have is correct because the postcondition of the program is the user's postcondition. Of course, we are also assuming the new operations work correctly.

Intended Semantics of the Abstractions

With each of the new operations we know the intended semantics, at least in terms of the local environment. Here are the two abstractions with their appropriate pre- and postconditions:

```
void GetPositive (int & V) {
    // Pre:  input stream == <v1,...,vN>    AND
    //       For I = 1,...,v(N-1): vI <= 0 AND
    //       vN > 0

    // Post: input stream == empty AND
    //       (out)V == vN              AND
    //       output stream ==
    //             N copies of the input prompt
}

void PrintPrimes (int N) {

    // Pre:  N > 0 AND

    // Post: output stream == (pre)output stream +
    //             p1
    //              .
    //              .
    //              .
    //             pvN          AND
    //           p1 == 2 is prime AND
    //           For I = 1,...,vN-1:
    //               p(I+1) is prime    AND
    //               For K = pI+1,...,p(I+1)-1:
    //                   K is not prime
}
```

Notice how the pre- and postconditions for these two abstractions help to define what is to be done in the yet-to-be-written code. Also recognize that we haven't just blindly put the pre- and postconditions for the calls into the abstraction definitions. One final point: Though it is often the case that specific reference to the input and output streams is omitted, when working from abstract to specific, it is helpful to be specific about the streams.

GetPositive

This shouldn't be difficult because we have seen problems like it before. In fact, GetPositive is a variation on the abstraction GetBounded from Section 7.4. The difference here is that we are interested in the effect of the loop on the input and output streams.

The postcondition for GetPositive can be produced by a rather simple unwinding process, where at each step a value is removed from the input stream and a copy of the prompt is put into the output stream as follows:

```
// Assert: input stream == <v1,...,vN>    AND
//         For I = 1,...,v(N-1): vI <= 0 AND
//         vN > 0
```

```
statement

// Assert: input stream == <v2,...,vN>     AND
//         V == v1                          AND
//         output stream == 1 copy of the prompt

// Assert: V == v1 <= 0          <<<---
statement

// Assert: input stream == <v3,...,vN>     AND
//         V == v2                          AND
//         output stream == 2 copies of the prompt

// Assert: V == v2 <= 0          <<<---
statement

// Assert: input stream == <v4,...,vN>     AND
//         V == v3                          AND
//         output stream == 3 copies of the prompt
```

There are two things to notice about this natural unwinding. First, the two assertions marked with "<<<---" are to indicate the failure of the validity condition. We don't want that as part of the main assertion, since after we read we don't immediately know if the new value is valid. Second, before the first **statement** no data has been read – so there can not be a check for validity. This subtle bit of information means that the first **statement** cannot be part of the repetition body.

At each step of the unwinding the effect of executing the statement is to display another input prompt and to read another value from the input stream. The code corresponding to **statement** is clearly the following:

```
cout << "Enter a positive value >> ";
cin  >> V;
```

At each point in the unwinding, the execution of this sequence will force the assertion that follows the sequence to be true.

By using the assertion variable (R), we can devise from this unwinding both a loop variant and a loop invariant. Knowing that the first prompt and read must precede the repetition leads us to the following asserted code for the abstraction GetPositive:

```
// Assert: input stream == <v1,...,vN>     AND
//         For I = 1,...,v(N-1): vI <= 0 AND
//         vN > 0                          AND

cout << "Enter a positive value >> ";
```

```
cin  >> V;

while // Variant: N - (R) - 1 >= 0
      // Invariant:
      //      input stream == <v((R)+1),...,vN> AND
      //      V == v(R)                          AND
      //      output stream == (R) copies of the prompt
      (V <= 0) {
      cout << "Enter a positive value >> ";
      cin >> V;  // Assert: loop variant decreases here!
}
// Assert: input stream == empty AND
//         V == vN > 0            AND
//         output stream == N copies of the input prompt
```

We're half done!

PrintPrimes

Now we turn our attention to the abstraction `PrintPrimes`. From the intended semantics we see that the parameter N is required to be a positive integer, and the abstraction has to display the first N prime numbers. To help us determine the code for this abstraction, we will first examine the postcondition which must be satisfied after the code has executed:

```
void PrintPrimes (int N) {

    // Pre:  N > 0

    // Post: output stream == (in)output stream +
    //                 p1
    //                  .
    //                  .
    //                  .
    //                 pvN             AND
    //         For I = 1,...,vN:   pI is prime
    //             AND
    //         For I = 1,...,vN-1:
    //             For K = pI+1,...,p(I+1)-1:
    //                 K is not prime
}
```

We know how to satisfy the first part of the postcondition – there must be a statement which prints out a number when it is found to be prime. The last three lines of the postcondition give the clue to how to generate the primes.

The final three lines are written as a nested guarded command. When confronted by such a condition, it is often a good idea to think "nested repetition." Then we should look to the outer condition for the outer loop invariant. If we think about an unwinding, the problem is easy:

```
initialization; // Val == 2 is p1 -- print it

// Assert:  nothing before p1 was a prime
//          output stream == p1 AND

statement;  // Val == p2 is produced and printed

// Assert:  Val == p2 is prime AND
//          nothing before p1 is prime AND
//          nothing between p1 and p2 is prime
//          output stream == p1   p2    AND

statement;  // Val == p3 is produced and printed

// Assert:  Val == p3 is prime AND
//          nothing before p1 is prime           AND
//          nothing between p1 and p2 is prime AND
//          nothing between p2 and p3 is prime
//          output stream == p1   p2   p3        AND
```

This unwinding gives us a lead on a loop invariant that says each value produced so far is a prime and between consecutive values there are no other primes. We restate this as the following logical condition:

```
For I=1,...,C:    pI is prime AND
For I=1,...,C-1: For K = pI+1,...,p(I+1)-1:
                         K is not prime
output stream == p1   ...   pC
```

Notice that this even makes sense after the first prime is produced, since the second "For I=1" clause is true when C is one.

The loop variant decreases each time we count another prime – i.e., as C gets closer to N. Here is the asserted loop:

```
Val = 2;
cout << Val << endl;

C = 1;
while // Variant: C <= N
     // Invariant: Val == pC AND
     //            For I=1,...,C: pI is prime     AND
     //            For I=1,...,C-1:
     //                For K = pI+1,...,p(I+1)-1:
     //                    K is not prime         AND
     //                output stream == p1   ...   pC
     (C < N) {
     statement;
```

```
        C = C + 1;    // Assert: invariant decreases here
   }
   // Assert: For I=1,...,N: pI is prime      AND
   //           For I=1,...,N-1:
   //               For K = pI+1,...,p(I+1)-1:
   //                   K is not prime         AND
   //           output stream == p1   ...   pN
```

Now we focus on **statement**, which is responsible for finding the value **Val** of the next prime and printing it out. Putting this another way, it is responsible for making the outer loop invariant true again. Since the variable **C** is incremented at the bottom of the loop, **statement** is responsible for making the phrase **Val == pC** true and the phrase

```
For K = pI+1,...,p(I+1)-1:
        K is not prime
```

true in the loop invariant for the case of **I == C-1** – in other words, for the gap of integers between **p(C-1)** and the new prime **pC == Val**. If we think of **Val** as stepping through the sequence of integers and identifying those which are primes, then we can modify the phrase above to become a loop invariant. The idea is that at anytime during the execution of the loop in **statement** numbers less than **Val** are known to be not prime. This implies the following loop invariant:

```
For K = pC+1,...,Val-1:
        K is not prime
```

The loop variant would just be the distance from **Val** to **p(I+1)** – that's a bit non-specific, but we know that there is a next prime, and if we keep incrementing **Val** we will run into it. So we can imagine replacing **statement** in our loop to produce the following code:

```
Val = 2;
cout << Val << endl;

C = 1;
while // Variant: C <= N
     // Invariant: Val == pC AND
     //              For I=1,...,C: pI is prime      AND
     //              For I=1,...,C-1:
     //                  For K = pI+1,...,p(I+1)-1:
     //                      K is not prime          AND
     //              output stream == p1   ...   pC
     (C < N) {
     Val = Val + 1;
```

```
        while // Variant: Val <= p(C+1)
              // Invariant: For K = pC+1,...,Val-1:
              //                    K is not prime
              (!prime(Val))
                  Val = Val + 1;  // Assert:  the loop variant
                                  //              decreases here
        // Assert: Val is prime == p(C+1)
        //          For K = pC+1,...,p(C_1)-1:
        //              K is not prime
        cout << Val << endl;

        C = C + 1;  // Assert:  the loop variant
                    //              decreases here
    }
    // Assert: For I=1,...,N: pI is prime      AND
    //          For I=1,...,N-1:
    //              For K = pI+1,...,p(I+1)-1:
    //                  K is not prime          AND
    //              output stream == p1   ...   pN
```

Termination

So far we have satisfied the first clause in the definition of program verification. What remains is to show that each of the abstractions used in the program will terminate. Since each of our abstractions has a loop in it, we need only show that each of these loops always terminates. Remember that we have already analyzed IsPrime and know it will terminate. We turn to the other two abstractions:

GetPositive Terminates

Here is the code for the loop in GetPositive. Notice that the loop variant is identified as N-(R)-1. (All other assertions have been stripped to clarify the situation.)

```
// Assert: input stream == <v1,...,vN>   AND
//          For I = 1,...,v(N-1): vI <= 0 AND
//              vN > 0                     AND

cout << "Enter a positive value >> ";
cin  >> V;

while // Variant: N - (R) - 1 >= 0
      (V <= 0) {
      cout << "Enter a positive value >> ";
      cin  >> V;  // Assert: loop variant decreases here!
}
```

We assume two things. First, the Nth input value is the first valid value – the loop must execute (N-1) times before reaching this valid value. Second, the virtual variable (R) increases on each pass through the loop. The cin statement, as its assertion implies, guarantees that on each pass through the loop the value read into V will be the one numbered (R)+1. This shows the loop will run the required number of times and when the last value has been entered the loop condition will fail. The abstraction GetPositive will always terminate.

PrintPrimes Terminates

```
    C = 1;
    while // Variant: C <= N
          (C < N) {
          Val = Val + 1;
          while // Variant: Val <= p(C+1)
                (!prime(Val))
                Val = Val + 1;  // Assert:  the loop variant
                                //              decreases here
          cout << Val << endl;

          C = C + 1;  // Assert:  the loop variant
                      //              decreases here
    }
```

Showing the termination of this loop is also easy and counts on the mathematical fact that the prime numbers are unbounded – i.e., whichever prime you have, there is always a larger one. This fact plus the fact that Val is incremented implies that the inner loop will terminate. Since the inner loop will terminate, we know that on each pass through the outer loop the value of C is incremented. Since it starts at 1 and the value of N is at least 1, by incrementing C it will eventually reach the value of N, at which time the outer loop will terminate. This code will always terminate.

Program Verified!

In this section we have worked through the verification of a simple but nontrivial program. We started by writing down the user pre- and postconditions for the program and then turned to verify two things: the inherent semantics of the program matches the intended semantics and the program will terminate regardless of the input (assuming a valid input value is eventually entered). By looking carefully at the assertions dictated by the statement semantics, studied in depth in the previous lessons, we were able to carry out the two tasks. The program indeed is correct.

One important point not to miss. You might have wondered why it is necessary to show termination after we went to all that trouble with loop invariants. If you look back to the fully asserted version of PrintPrimes, consider how things change if we remove the following line:

```
    Val = Val + 1;
```

In this case, the loop never terminates because the loop variant never changes. Suppose in addition we start `Val` at 24 rather than 2 – we want to see the primes after 24. Then we find that even though the loop never terminates, the loop variant remains true on each loop pass.

Appendix A

Logic

Our persuasive style of programming hinges on the use of assertions, i.e., Boolean expressions. The lessons in this text rely heavily on the reader's ability to simplify and manipulate assertions that are sometimes simple, other times quite complex. The purpose of this appendix is to give a very basic overview of formal logic, the mathematical theory upon which Boolean expressions are based. In the sections that follow we will discuss the basic properties of the three logical operations (and, or, not), see what it means to say that two Boolean expressions are equivalent, explore standard algebraic properties (associativity, distributivity, commutativity) for the logical operations, and finally investigate how to carry out various simplifications and manipulations of example expressions.

A.1   The Logical Operations and Truth Tables

There are three standard logical (i.e., Boolean) operations: $\wedge$ (and), $\vee$ (or), $\neg$ (not). Because these operations are applied to the set of Boolean values (true, false), it is easy to specify these operations by listing the outcome of every possible computation.

$\neg$	
true	false
false	true

$\wedge$	true	false
true	true	false
false	false	false

$\vee$	true	false
true	true	true
false	true	false

An alternative approach to defining the logical operations is to use a *truth table*. Suppose we look at a simple expression such as $(A \wedge \text{true})$. We use a truth table to show every possible computational result for this expression. Since A can have only two values, there can be only two computational results for this expression. We display the truth table as follows:

A	$A \wedge \text{true}$
true	true
false	false

This same technique can, of course, be used to determine values for more complex expressions. The expression $A \vee (B \wedge A)$ has the following truth table:

A	B	$B \wedge A$	$A \vee (B \wedge A)$
true	true	true	true
true	false	false	true
false	true	false	false
false	false	false	false

Actually, the third column could be left out, but it is there to make it easier to fill in the final column. This is a common technique with truth tables, as you will see in later sections.

Truth tables also give an alternative mechanism for defining the basic Boolean operations. Here we combine the truth tables for the three operations into one table. Notice that doing this makes some of the entries for $\neg A$ redundant.

A	B	$\neg A$	$A \wedge B$	$A \vee B$
true	true	false	true	true
true	false	false	false	true
false	true	true	false	true
false	false	true	false	false

The idea underlying the truth table is for each row to represent a unique state for the variables in the expression. If there are two variables, then there are four possible states, three variables have eight states, n variables have 2^n states. We will see in the next section how we can use the truth table idea to identify equivalent expressions.

A.2   Expression Equivalence

Two Boolean expressions are equivalent if they have the same truth tables – i.e., they always evaluate to the same value given the same state. To indicate A and B are equivalent we write $A \equiv B$.

Example 31 $- A \vee (\neg A \wedge B) \equiv A \vee B$
▼

We use truth tables to show the following equivalence is true:

$$A \vee (\neg A \wedge B) \equiv A \vee B$$

To do this we set up a table with four rows (since there are two variables) and the left columns with the four possible states for the variables.

A	B	$(\neg A \wedge B)$	$A \vee (\neg A \wedge B)$	$A \vee B$
true	true	false	true	true
true	false	false	true	true
false	true	true	true	true
false	false	false	false	false

Notice that the first column on the right (headed by $(\neg A \wedge B)$) is present to clarify the evaluation of the expression $A \vee (\neg A \wedge B)$. Then we notice the values in the last two columns on the right have the same sequences of values and conclude the two expressions are in fact equivalent.

▲

The big advantage to identifying equivalent expressions is for manipulating and simplifying expressions: in particular, if $A \equiv B$ and A is a subexpression of E, then replacing A in E by B yields another expression equivalent to E. We will look at the consequences of this substitution principle in the last section of this appendix. We have put this substitution principle to good use in Lesson 12 (see especially Section 12.5).

Here are two more truth tables that illustrate the notion of equivalence:

Example 32 $- \neg\neg A \equiv A$
▼

A	$\neg A$	$\neg\neg A$	A
true	false	true	true
false	true	false	false

▲

Example 33 $- A \wedge (B \vee C) \equiv (A \wedge B) \vee (A \wedge C)$
▼

A	B	C	$(B \vee C)$	$(A \wedge B)$	$(A \wedge C)$	$A \wedge (B \vee C)$
true	true	true	true	true	true	true
true	true	false	true	true	false	true
true	false	true	true	false	true	true
true	false	false	false	false	false	false
false	true	true	true	false	false	false
false	true	false	true	false	false	false
false	false	true	true	false	false	false
false	false	false	false	false	false	false

A	B	C	$(A \land B) \lor (A \land C)$
true	true	true	true
true	true	false	true
true	false	true	true
true	false	false	false
false	true	true	false
false	true	false	false
false	false	true	false
false	false	false	false

▲

The equivalences in the previous two examples are well known and important enough to be given names. Here follows a listing of some of the more important named equivalences for Boolean expressions:

Negation Rule $\neg\neg A \equiv A$

De Morgan's Rules $\neg(A \land B) \equiv \neg A \lor \neg B$
                         $\neg(A \lor B) \equiv \neg A \land \neg B$

Identity Rules $A \land \neg A \equiv \text{false}$
                         $A \land \text{true} \equiv A$
                         $A \lor \neg A \equiv \text{true}$
                         $A \lor \text{false} \equiv A$

Associative Rules $A \land (B \land C) \equiv (A \land B) \land C$
                         $A \lor (B \lor C) \equiv (A \lor B) \lor C$

Distributive Rules $A \land (B \lor C) \equiv (A \land B) \lor (A \land C)$
                         $A \lor (B \land C) \equiv (A \lor B) \land (A \lor C)$

It makes a good exercise to verify these equivalences – just apply the truth table techniques illustrated in the previous two examples.

A.3   Simplification of Boolean Expressions

In this section we will look at several examples of expression simplification and also manipulation. Some of these examples are used in various lessons in the text – references will be given when appropriate. Notice that in proving these equivalences we do not make use of truth tables. Rather, we use substitution, making use of the equivalences in the rules above or other equivalences which we have derived.

Example 34 $- A \lor B \equiv A \lor (\neg A \land B)$

▼

We want to show the following equivalence holds:

$$A \lor B \equiv A \lor (\neg A \land B)$$

We can see this equivalence if we follow the following sequence of equivalences – notice that we start with the left-hand side of the desired equivalence:

$$
\begin{aligned}
A \lor (\neg A \land B) &\equiv (A \lor \neg A) \land (A \lor B) && \lor \text{ distributes over } \land \\
&\equiv \textbf{true} \land (A \lor B) && X \lor \neg X \equiv \textbf{true} \\
&\equiv A \lor B && \textbf{true} \land X \equiv X
\end{aligned}
$$

(See Lesson 12.5 for an application of this equivalence.)

▲

Example 35 $- \neg(A \lor \neg B) \equiv \neg A \land B$

▼

Proof of the equivalence proceeds as follows:

$$
\begin{aligned}
\neg(A \lor \neg B) &\equiv \neg A \land \neg\neg B && \text{De Morgan's rule on } \lor \\
&\equiv \neg A \land B && \text{Negation rule}
\end{aligned}
$$

▲

Example 36 $- (X \land Y \land Z) \lor (A \land Y \land B) \equiv Y \land ((X \land Z) \lor (A \land B))$

▼

This equivalence hinges on the use of the commutative property of $\land$ (step 1 below) and on a backward application of the distributive property of $\land$ over $\lor$ (step 2 below).

$$
\begin{aligned}
(X \land Y \land Z) \lor (A \land Y \land B) &\equiv (Y \land X \land Z) \lor (Y \land A \land B) \\
&\equiv Y \land ((X \land Z) \lor (A \land B))
\end{aligned}
$$

(See Lesson 12.5 for an application of this equivalence.)

▲

Index